Legal Certainty in Real Estate Transactions

A Comparison of England and France

Editors:
Bertrand du Marais
and David Marrani

Legal Certainty in Real Estate Transactions

A Comparison of England and France

intersentia

METRO

Ius Commune Europaeum

Intersentia Ltd
Sheraton House | Castle Park
Cambridge | CB3 0AX | United Kingdom
Tel.: +44 1223 370 170 | Fax: +44 1223 370 169
Email: mail@intersentia.co.uk
www.intersentia.com | www.intersentia.co.uk

Distribution for the UK and Ireland:
NBN International
Airport Business Centre, 10 Thornbury Road
Plymouth, PL6 7 PP
United Kingdom
Tel.: +44 1752 202 301 | Fax: +44 1752 202 331
Email: orders@nbninternational.com

Distribution for Europe and all other countries:
Intersentia Publishing nv
Groenstraat 31
2640 Mortsel
Belgium
Tel.: +32 3 680 15 50 | Fax: +32 3 658 71 21
Email: mail@intersentia.be

Distribution for the USA and Canada:
International Specialized Book Services
920 NE 58th Ave. Suite 300
Portland, OR 97213
USA
Tel.: +1 800 944 6190 (toll free) | Fax: +1 503 280 8832
Email: info@isbs.com

Legal Certainty in Real Estate Transactions: A Comparison of England and France

ISBN 978-1-78068-298-3
D/2016/7849/139
NUR 822

British Library Cataloguing in Publication Data. A catalogue record for this book is available from the British Library.

CONTENTS

INTRODUCTION

INTRODUCTION

Bertrand du Marais
David Marrani

COMPARING LEGAL CERTAINTY IN FRANCE AND ENGLAND

1. How to Assess the Legal Framework Used to Secure Real Estate Transactions in France and England?

This research has been launched in reaction to the assessment of property registration law published in the World Bank Doing Business reports (DB). The research team was chaired by Bertrand du Marais[1], Marie-France Nicolas[2] and David Marrani.[3] The aim of the research was to identify the methodology of a rigorous and comparative assessment of the legal certainty produced by French and English law, pertaining to real estate properties with professional use. Like the DB reports, this work is one of the rare legal impact assessments dealing with real estate property focused on real estate properties with professional use.

This comparative research was carried out simultaneously in France and England by a multidisciplinary academic team, with the assistance of practitioners, composed on the one hand, of lawyers, and on the other hand, of economists and management specialists.[4] The "GIP Mission de recherche "Droit et Justice"", in the framework of the Economic Attractiveness of Law Program[5] sponsored this research.

1 Conseiller d'Etat, Chairman of the Think Tank FIDES (http://fides.u-paris10.fr), seconded as Public Law Professor to Université Paris Ouest Nanterre La Défense, co-chair of the Masters in Law – Economics at the time of the research.

2 Maître de conférences honoraire (Emeritus Assistant Professor) in Private Law, Université Paris Ouest Nanterre La Défense.

3 Director of the Institute of Law, Jersey, Senior Lecturer in Law, University of Essex at the time of the research.

4 In France: under the supervision of Marie-France Nicolas and Bertrand du Marais, lawyers, were involved: Jean-Sylvestre Bergé, Camille Bourdaire, Aurore Chaigneau, lawyers, Régis Lanneau, lawyer and economist; Christian Schmidt (for the initial phase of the research) and Philippe Frouté, economists. In the United Kingdom: under the supervision of David Marrani, lawyers, were involved: Youseph Farah, Peter Luther, Marios Koutsia and Alan Moran, lawyers. This team of academics benefited from the experience of practitioners: Me C. Deneuville, *notaire* in France, and A. Moran, solicitor in England.

5 Under the chairmanship of B. du Marais, this research programme carried out, between 2004 and 2007, a thorough assessment of the results and methodology of the Doing Business Reports.

The team work is described in this introduction along with the major findings of the research in a policy oriented way for the use of policy makers (especially the ministry of Justice) and of the relevant professions (especially the *notariat*).

The main operational lessons from the research are threefold:

- From a methodological point of view, in order to measure the economic impact of law;
- From a scientific point of view, about the role of *notaires* when dealing with real estate transactions on real estate properties with professional use of significant value;
- From a strategic point of view, about the future of the current organization of the French *notaires*.

2. The irrelevance of the *Doing Business* methodology

The comparative description of the legal framework used in the two legal systems, as well as the practices in real business life, demonstrates that it is impossible to sequence such a transaction in order to assess the efficiency of law.

However, and for each country under review, the Doing Business reports are based on the synthetic quantitative index of "the ease of doing business". This index is the unweighted average of about ten sub-indicators.[6] Each of these sub-indicators is supposed to assess the impact of the country legal framework on a specific function of the firm or on its development stages.

Each of these sub-indicators is itself a combination of indexes built according to three types of measurements: either a binary coding of the existing legislation, or a computation, according to a "time and motion", Taylor like approach, of time and number of steps to complete a specific legal transaction; or the official cost of these operations [See du Marais et al., 2006, Ménard et du Marais, 2006].

The Doing Business reports include a sub-indicator for "registering property" for which France got its lowest ranking.

As a matter of fact, especially during the earlier Doing Business reports, France climbed in the general ranking from 47th in the 2006 report (first report to publish the global ranking) to 31st in the 2008 report, up to 26th in the 2011 report. This was the result of an improvement in almost all sub-indicators.[7] France decreased to the 29th position in the 2012 report.

On the contrary, its ranking for the "registering property" sub-indicator has always been very mediocre, from 144th in the 2005 report to 149th in the 2012 report while decreasing down to 166th in the 2009 edition. This "registering property" sub-indicator exerts clearly a negative pressure on the overall result of France. The problem is that the

6 To the 5 initial sub-indicators, this research program carried out, between 2004 and 2007, a theory assessment of the results and methodology of the Doing Business Reports.

7 The change in a country's ranking is both due to the "improvement" of the country's results but also to the broadening of the data base to new countries. The Doing Business team adjusts the ranking to a similar sample only for the next report.

Doing Business data are used as raw material for other rankings or assessment, e.g. the financial rating agency [du Marais et al., 2007].

On the contrary, Great-Britain overall position in the Doing Business reports has always looked much better (9th in the 2006 report, 7th in the 2012 report), partly thanks to its good position for the "registering property" sub-indicator (around 23rd from the 2006 report to the 2009 report[8]).

This research confirms the existing criticisms ledged against the Doing Business methodology. It shows very clearly the great difficulty, if not the mere impossibility, of any legal "sequencing" of the different steps of a business transaction. These limitations apply here very clearly to the acquisition of a building with professional use [Bourdaire & Mignot, 2010].

Indeed, such business transaction should be assessed as a whole. Parties to the contract deal with such a transaction from a global point of view. Each of its functional steps interacts with each others and may be simultaneous.

3. The French *notaire* as an "integrator"

As part of the operations that were studied here, namely real estate transactions on real estate properties with professional use of significant value, this research presents a picture of the French *notaire* that is not well known. It shows in particular that the *notaire* in France acts as an "integrator", defraying some of the costs and involved in steps that are necessary to the parties to complete the transaction.

It confirms that in terms of cost, the competition that may exist between *notaires* on this market cannot be expressed by a modification of prices but by increasing services supplied. In the type of transactions analyzed, the *notaire* will pay for the various audits (due diligence) falling onto the parties. In terms of duration, it will conduct these audits during the period between the preliminary contract and closing.

Moreover, regarding the operations that have been studied here, the practitioners met are determined first by a financial logic, in which the return on capital, the capital gain expected and the logical distribution of a portfolio between the different real estate markets globally, are the main arguments of the demand for investment. To some extent, transaction costs are a second level constraint. As has been observed, operators do not perceive transaction costs as significantly different from either side of the Channel. Investors react in fact as if, once the decision to purchase has been taken for reasons of financial management, these transaction costs, including those related to reducing the uncertainty of the transaction were a non-discriminatory and exogenous variable.

In such transactions, both in terms of calculating the cost and time of the operation, our research shows that the intervention of the notaire is widely perceived as neutral to the eyes of the actors.

8 Before the United Kingdom stepped down to the 68th position for the "registering property" sub-indicator in the 2012 report, for reasons still unclear to the authors of the present study.

However, regarding again the impact of the legal framework on transaction costs in acquiring real estate, we should maybe seek the comparative effects of different legal systems in two other directions.

On the one hand, it would be interesting to compare the relative levels of certain direct costs, even non-monetary ones, involved in transaction costs, especially in the form of opportunity costs and costs related to uncertainty.

In the first sense, *the time* to materialize the agreement could be an opportunity cost to the extent that resources are, during this time, immobilised and unusable for other profitable purposes. Similarly, *uncertainty about the completion* of the transaction itself is a transaction cost imposing a risk on the parties, which can result in an increase in the cost of capital.

However, the comparison between the French and English legal frameworks shows precisely that in matters of real estate acquisition, there is a clear divergence, reflected by both an opportunity cost and uncertainty.

Thus there exists in France an asymmetry between the situation of the buyer and the seller that does not exist in English law. Therein, the acquisition is achieved in one step. Then again the purchaser shall engage upstream of closing with "due diligence" that can also last for several weeks. However, the sale is finally acquired from the parties' agreement.

However, the sale takes place in two stages in France, with a relatively long period between the preliminary contract and closing. Certainly this period, which generally corresponds to the average time to serve the right of first refusal, is used by the parties – and especially the *notaire* – to perform audits and diagnostics.

The time between, on the one hand, what we could identify as the consideration of the transaction by the purchaser and, secondly, the completion of the acquisition is, by in large, the same in both systems. However, this period is characterized by an asymmetry, in France, of the situations of the parties, since it is characterized by the commitment of the seller without commitment from the buyer.

It remains, however, in a subsequent research, to evaluate and quantify notably on the cost of capital, the effect of these two factors: dissociation into two stages and asymmetrical engagement of the vendor.

4. In a stretched European context, these results argue for the adoption of a new strategy for the French *notaire*

We know that the mandatory involvement of the *notaires*, as basis for an organisation of the real estate transactions described as "Latin notary", has been the subject of intense criticism from the mid-2000s. Particularly, the European institutions have criticized the way this system is regulated, uncompetitive and hence inefficient.

This question has been renewed in recent times, with several rulings of the Court of Justice of the European Union. Indeed, with six rulings on the same day (ECJ, 24 May 2011, Commission v. C-50/08 France, c. Belgium 47/08 c. Luxembourg 51/08 c. Austria 53/08 c. Germany 54/08 and c. Greece 61/08), the Court has permanently weakened the "Latin notary" (du Marais, 2011).

Certainly, the court simply ruled on the nationality requirement for access to the notarial profession, considered as contrary to the freedom of establishment and art. 43 TEC (49 TFEU) and not justified by "the exercise of public authority."

However, the scope, and perhaps even the target, of these six rulings go far beyond. Indeed, certain steps of the reasoning are drafted in very general terms, especially regarding the mission of "ensuring the legality and legal acts concluded between individuals. However, only the pursuit of this objective cannot justify the powers necessary to this end available only to *notaires* nationals of the Member State concerned. (Paragraph 85). "

Since the bodies of *notaires* were directly involved in the research program on "Economic Attractiveness of Law", it may be interesting to learn from this research, in this context, some strategic conclusions.

Moreover, beyond the notariat itself, we must remember that this is a centrepiece of Government intervention in France who would be covered by the banalisation of legal services applicable to real estate acquisitions through the Caisse des Dépôts et Consignations that centralizes notaries' deposits. The challenge is for the French economy, systemic.

First, we may recommend an argument centered on the differentiation of *notaires* in terms of quality rather than in terms of price.

Indeed, and secondly, if we extend the results of this research, it leads to even think, that the liberalization of the notariat would, for the type of transactions analysed in this research, have very little impact on prices. As a matter of fact, the notaire is competitive as far as we may compare it with the English system if we consider, firstly, the whole operation and secondly, all the various audits and procedures that must be taken into consideration by the parties and that the *notaire* incorporates and take into account.

Third, this research suggests that the defence of the French notariat could also go through rigorous and quantified analysis on how *notaires* can fit into a logic of economic regulation, in terms of cost and service offered. Recent cases of the EUCJ encouraged to develop a specific argumentation about the Latin notary in terms of Community law of SGEI: on pricing, universal service and regulation, particularly.

5. References

Banque Mondiale - World Bank, 2003. *Doing Business in 2004: Understanding Regulation.* World Bank and Oxford, University Press, Washington DC.

Banque Mondiale - World Bank, 2004. *Doing Business in 2005: Removing Obstacles to Growth,* World Bank and Oxford University Press, Washington DC.

Banque Mondiale - World Bank, 2005. *Doing Business in 2006: Creating Jobs.* World Bank and Oxford University Press, Washington DC.

Banque Mondiale - World Bank, 2006. *Doing Business in 2007: How to Reform.* World Bank and Oxford University Press, Washington DC.

Banque Mondiale - World Bank, 2010. *Doing Business in 2011: Making a difference for entrepreneurs,* World Bank and Oxford University Press, Washington DC.

Banque Mondiale, 2011, *Doing Business en 2012: Entreprendre dans un monde plus transparent,* World Bank and Oxford University Press, Washington DC.

Bourdaire-Mignot C. et Chaigneau A. (2010), "Pourquoi mesurer l'efficacité des transactions immobilières en France?", *La Semaine Juridique Notariale et Immobilière,* no. 37, 17 Septembre 2010, 1273.

du Marais B. (sous dir.),. Blanchet D. et Dorbec A., (2006), *Des indicateurs pour mesurer le droit? Les limites méthodologiques des rapports* Doing Business, Paris, La Documentation française, coll. "Perspectives sur la justice", 2006.

du Marais B. (2011), "La CJUE fragilise durablement le notariat latin" en jugeant que la condition de nationalité méconnaît la liberté d'établissement et n'est pas justifiée par "l'exercice de l'autorité publique" obs. sur CJUE, 24 mai 2011, Commission c/ France, aff. C-50/08, *Concurrences,* Chronique secteur public, N° 3-2011, pp. 209–210.

Ménard C.; du Marais, B., (2006). "Can We Rank Legal Systems According to Their Economic Efficiency?" In: Peter Nobel and Marina Gets (Eds.), *New Frontiers of Law and Economics.* Zürich, Schulthess, pp. 7–27.

David Marrani*

INTRODUCTORY REMARKS ON COMPARATIVE LAW AND INTERDISCIPLINARITY

1. This project was ambitious. Not only because of the scope of the research undertaken, but also because it aimed to consider multiples and mixed approaches of different legal cultures. It is therefore fundamental in my opinion to analyse some ideas on the operation comparison itself in the context of an inter disciplinary work, which we have undertaken here, to really try to understand or at least grasp what is at stake in this project.

We should primarily keep in mind the debates surrounding legal systems, legal cultures and legal traditions. Within the debate, culture, or (sometimes) its very close 'ally', tradition, have become a crucial notion. The idea of culture in general and legal culture in particular, gives a large place to memory, a social memory conceptualized as a sort of super ego, a sort of entanglement of heideggerian temporality combining time, chronology of past, present and future.

There are of course types of societies that are traditional and some non-traditional. The main point for us here has to be the law itself, as it connects to these conceptions. Each type of society faces a certain type of law, and the matter escalates when we link those points to the classical divide tradition and modernity, but also its Enlightenments' derivative, the new rearranged divide tradition and rationality.

For Western Europe (or Western European and country) and its tradition of comparison (Twinnings) in civil law tradition, there are according to Glenn elements of traditional chtonic and talmudic that give clues about why and where some legal definitions are coming from, opening our eyes to what are specific legal identities. In the common law tradition, it all derives, again for Glenn, from an accident resulting from the conquest of England by the Normans. The smallest common denominators, important elements of the comparison, are definitely the alleged core of the ancient traditions. On the one hand, in common law, we have the use of oral "through the accumulation of precedent," creating "a body of common experience" through memory/ies.[1] On the other hand, in Southern Europe, the civil law tradition, appears rooted in writings, in the tradition of chthonic and Talmudic, as explained by Glenn, that goes much deeper than the rational explanation of roots located in the writings of Roman

* Institute of Law, Jersey.

1 Glenn, P, *Legal Traditions of the World*, Oxford OUP 3rd ed 2007, esp. p. 125. According to Glenn, there is a written Torah and an oral Torah that has become written, pp. 238–239.

Empire, through the codex.[2] The multiple consequences of this divide serve as a foundation for an obvious binary tandem secrecy / transparency.

According to Legrand, the two traditions represented in Western Europe that the English consider "civil law" and "common law" interact under the Treaty of Rome.[3] These two traditions remain consistent discursive creations, sufficiently homogeneous that they can be considered as independent. Basically these two visions define two ways of understanding reality (in the sense of 'the world)', and operate as mirrors of two mythological bases.[4]

Borrowing comments made by professor Samuel, comparison can be seen as a hermeneutic exercise, where 'the job of the comparatist is not simply to compare rules since these are nothing more than a strings of words; they are the surface appearance of the law.'[5] The text of the rules just touches the substance or the surface, the appearance of the rule. Indeed, 'What the comparatist must do is get below their surface in order to discover the cultural *mentalité* that these rules express. It is not the rule itself that should be the focus of comparison but what the rule signifies in terms of political, social, economic and ideological context from which it has emerged.'[6] It is in other words, on the legal culture of a society that a rule appears, according to what Legrand called *mentalité*, or deep cognitive structure. A rule 'means', 'signifies' in a specific economic, political, social, ideological context, exogenous factors that determine the law as it appears. In its appropriation of Berthlot's hermeneutic, Samuel describes a scheme different than the traditional functional approach. In the traditional functional approach, there is a 'quest for a positive truth attaching to the existence of this or that rule.'[7] The difference between functional and hermeneutical, is mainly the idea of a vertical relationship between two elements: A the signified (what is expressed, ie the cultural mentality) and B the signifier (what is, ie the rule). These elements interact constantly with the help of internalized *mentalités*, internal engine of legal cultures. Comparative law becomes a structural exercise, which is characterized by elements that become signs, elements of a system (not in the meaning of legal system), operating as a code. A signifies while compared to B, C, in opposition to it. The difference then between civil law and common law would solely be that there is an operation of a classification in civil law, axiomatic, virtual, while common law would have no classification, and would be non axiomatic. Civil law would be a symmetry which cannot be broken while common law could be.

According to Samuel again, the common law's main character is complexity. Its structure is complex and revolves around signifiers serving a list of remedies and causes of actions, in the surface, in the text of the judgments.

2 Ibid.

3 Legrand, P., 'How to Compare Now'", 2 *Legal studies*, 16, 1996, pp. 232–242, esp. p. 232.

4 Ibid., p. 240.

5 Samuel, G., 'Epistemology and Comparative Law', in Van Hoecke, M., (ed.) *Epistemology and Methodology of Comparative Law*, Oxford Hart 2004, pp. 35–77, esp. pp. 60–61.

6 Ibid.

7 Ibid.

It appears therefore that what becomes very important is to consider the other in its view of the law, and to be very careful of what we do as

> 'civilians think they understand the common law, but in failing to indulge in serious hermeneutical investigation, " the comparatist"...does not realise that the common law of England operates on the basis of epistemological assumption which are hidden behind the judicial decision or the statute and which determine then, and these assumptions distinguish in a fundamental way the common law tradition from the civil law world.'

Perhaps, we also need to keep in mind, following Lombardi, recently celebrated in the previously cited work of Richard, that we ought to take into account that comparison is a second level of research that appears to be structured around a specific discourse, that of the discipline in which this discourse is embedded.[8]

2. According to Örücü, 'to talk of 'comparability' may evoke an intellectual activity of juxtaposing somewhat similar systems, institutions or rules.'[9] Comparative law would then appears as something that brings us above something. It becomes clear that comparing is therefore about crossing something, moving from one side to another, passing over a 'gap'. Comparative law is about comparing two (or more) systems, cultures or traditions: it is about talking, speaking, debating and writing of and on the 'in between' of the law, even though we know that according to our partisan choice (system, culture, tradition) we are doing the 'same' comparison. That said, comparative law is not solely concerned with theoretical matter, it also deals, as we have seen with Samuel, with the methods.[10] Örücü explains that:

> 'Another concern is which methods can and should be used by comparative lawyers. Is there a standard comparative law methodology? Apart from regarding comparison itself as a method, the problems of comparative legal methodology are very varied and have been discussed in different ways by many comparative lawyers.'[11]

What seems to become clear in fact, is that there are no strict methods in comparative work:

> 'Although comparative law research is open ended – the methodology being dictated by the strategy of the comparative lawyer – and there is no standard methodology, the possibility of comparison is dependent upon the existence and availability of data.'[12]

8 Richard, P., *Le Jeu de la Différence, Réflexions sur l'Epistémologie du Droit Comparé*, Laval Pul, Dikè 2007, pp. 117–120. My translation.

9 Örücü, E., 'Developing Comparative Law', in Örücü, E. and Nelken, D., (eds), *Comparative Law a handbook*, Oxford Hart 2007, pp. 43–66, esp. p. 48.

10 See Glaner about the possibility of absence of methods.

11 Örücü, E., 'Developing Comparative Law', p. 48.

12 Ibid., pp. 48–49.

The idea of strategy is perfectly intellectually viable. We need to do what we can and what is appropriate at a point of time, and space, for a specific object of study. But there is another dilemma that needs to be taken care of: the divide public law/private law. This divide goes with another nature of comparative law, about comparative law of an 'articulated discourse'.[13] It is quite obvious that the two have separated objectives. Public law appears to privilege the search for differences surrounding national discourses. Private law, on the other hand, searches for the convergence and the establishment of a 'common' law. So how does this work with comparative law, if we consider comparison as a crossing in between 'things', meaning an operation of opening up onto the others, and therefore an intellectual work of respecting identity as alterity. Many comparative methods take into account the divide when dealing with issues related to private or public law while comparing. Quite often, comparative studies undertaken are in fact dealing with a specific legal domain.[14] What matters for the comparatist is to develop ideas concerning sometimes 'public law' and sometimes, maybe more often (like in the case of this collective work) 'private law'. From that perspective, comparing seems to be an answer to a characteristic epistemological imperative. It is structured around a specific discourse, the one of the discipline in which this discourse is incorporated. This reasoning appears logical in academia where *par nature*, the division between 'public lawyers' and 'private lawyers' has become the 'fundamental' division, a prior imperative to any lawyer becoming a comparative lawyer: a comparative lawyer is first a public or a private lawyer before becoming a comparative lawyer. This methodological imperative was for instance analysed by Lombardi as explained by Richard. In his opinion, two methodological levels exist that can be used by lawyers. The general level concerns comparison '*lato sensu*' and a second level, a specific sector of legal experience.[15]

Therefore comparative public law and comparative private law should (pre) suppose their own methodology. Lombardi considers that analysing the logic of the instrumental function inherent to the comparative reasoning is a necessity.[16] We must distinguish on one side the 'formants' that will be required according to the domain of comparison, and on the other side the final objectives of comparison. The formants which are used in the implementation of comparison are different whether we are 'in' private law or 'in' public law. As a consequence, for a private lawyer, the study of norms and cases will prevail, with legislation, doctrine and case law and perhaps sometimes economics, as taming point of the discourse (issue that are relevant to our work here). For public law, the process is of different nature, because of the social relationships, the level of the 'group' and the law resulting. Societies are certainly, for most of us, actual living organisms and their constitutions is the core, again, for most of us, of any political regime, and therefore can be subject to several distortions caused by practice. For Lombardi, there is something else. That something else is what makes up the spirit of a

13 Richard, P., *Le Jeu de la Différence, Réflexions sur l'Epistémologie du Droit Comparé*, Laval Pul Dike 2007, pp. 117–122, esp. p. 117.

14 See on legal domain the work of Matthew Dyson, 'Legal Domains and Comparative Law', *The Edinburgh Law Review* 17.3 (2013), pp. 420–430.

15 Richard, *Jeu de la différence*, esp. p. 118.

16 Ibid., esp. pp. 118–119.

system. To take such steps is of course very courageous and maybe even dangerous because the comparatist may then go beyond the boundaries of law. He or she may enter the sphere of political metaphysics and 'pollute' law. Comparative studies 'in' public law, are, by definition, more focused on differences than those 'in' private law. Private law, is more concerned with the relationships between natural and legal persons of private laws, and deals predominantly more naturally with the similarities between legal systems (adequately used here) and norms as well as the establishment of a kind of new *jus commune*. On the contrary, public law is fundamentally different: each State has develop its own political equation, its own national or even nationalistic discourse, and aims to become a reference, that is a place where is staged the theatrical scene of the normative principle that should be used (even though the ECHR preamble states the emergence of common constitutional elements).

There is obviously a close relationship between law and civilization. Richard explains, that for instance Latinity left us as heritage of the 13th and the 14Th centuries, the words 'civil' and 'civilization'.[17] The French civil code has in that sense a flavour of 'civilising', an operation that mirrors in the 'real' society the too philosophical 1789 Declaration. The codification appears at that point as an evolution of the relationship between the State and the civil society, that permits the separation between 'private sphere' and 'public sphere': private relations are now based (theoretically) on a contract between autonomous individuals. Codification began a system of rules guarantying the 'private sphere' from the interference of the 'public sphere'. The *Code civil* appears to be a document protecting the fundamental freedoms of the new actors of post 1789 revolution French society. The ritualisation imposed by the State through the use of positive law enables to sustain a conversation between individuals. But what is witnessed is the intra-state conversation, that is becoming more and more trans-national (including European law, which is based on a similar logic) rather than inter-states. This seems to be the result of the development of new types of society or new analysis of society such as the Risk Society for example. Consequently, this situation requires the establishment of a 'common' civil law allowing trade. 'Integration law' was thus initially engendered by the growth of an international sectorial integrative organization with mainly an economic vocation in accordance with a functionalist reasoning. This process, which concerns private law, tends to highlight the relationships between norms rather than their differences. Consecutively, what is traditionally understood as 'comparative law' allows the perception of a uniformed legal space in the social space, process which concerns the development of comparative contract law, comparative company law, comparative family law, … (we should also keep in mind that civilians assume they understand the common law however they most of the time do not). In addition, the apparent convergence between civil law and common law may not be as evident as it seems or is exposed. It may not *be* happening at all. Then again, a common common law might emerge rather than a common civil law.

17 Ibid., p. 120.

3. Our collective work is on a comparison between legal certainty and *sécurité juridique*. It is on what is happening not only in the area of certainty and/or *sécurité*, considering whether these are not the same but at least similar, comparable, 'things' that are assumed to be equal but in different traditions.[18] Writing about a legal tradition is always a complex exercise. Comparing two legal traditions is an even more difficult one. When the traditions are separated by a long-lasting physical and historical gap, it becomes perilous. And that is even trickier when facing people who think they know about the gap while actually knowing very little. The comparison in this book is concerned with what Legrand considers 'the two legal traditions represented in Western Europe – known to Anglophones as the "civil law" and the "common law".' A preliminary question should be why choosing to compare those traditions (instead of others)? One may want to believe that like Oedipus we should be able to give the correct answer in order to survive the Sphinx. One trivial answer perhaps lies in history. Indeed, these not only are the 'most common' traditions for us, western European lawyers, but they also correspond (nicely) to the classical and perhaps rather dated, to be fair, idea of major legal systems (systems being used in that case has a didactic tool rather than a conceptual one). Both traditions also relate to former major empires (the French and the British ones) that have exported their vision of the world through their specific visions of the law, hence their 'remaining' importance. That is perhaps the most important reasons for us, with the final one, that is according to Legrand, that both 'find themselves interacting with one another within a general legal framework, that of the Treaty of Rome'.[19]

Any research undertaken within the 'European laboratory' at some point can only highlight this interaction. Most of the time, comparatists aim to decipher the 'truth' in each legal tradition. Indeed if we consider these two legal traditions as 'discursive formations of sufficient homogeneity', we end up with evidence of sufficient homogeneity of each legal tradition that makes them 'autonomous discursivities' and permits ultimately to define 'two modes of understanding reality (reflecting the two foundational mythologies)'.[20] Comparative law is, fundamentally 'a commitment to interdisciplinary',[21] and we may suppose that this commitment obliges us to analyse beyond the legal sides of the matter, the problem of vocabulary generally and of legal vocabulary particularly. The action of comparing law interacts with a philological analysis of words in both legal traditions. Indeed, if we are looking at 'autonomous discursivitites', an important place has to be given to the issue of language,[22] that for Lacan incarnates historically communities, whether in France or in the UK.[23] As soon as a language exists, a concrete universe emerges and significations found their place within this universe, as the

18 Note that we will use traditions hereinafter.

19 Legrand, 'How to Compare Now', esp. p. 232.

20 Ibid., p. 240.

21 Ibid., p. 238.

22 Lacan declared that 'l'inconscient est structuré comme un language' (the unconscious is structured like a language) but also that 'l'inconscient est la condition de la linguistique' (language is the condition of linguistic). We know that Freud considered that the language was a 'thing' replacing another one. In Lacan, the priority is that second 'thing' that will become in his work the symbolic order.

23 Lacan, J., *Le Séminaire, tome 2: Le Moi dans la Théorie de Freud et dans la Technique de la Psychoanalyse, 1954–1955,* Paris Seuil 1978, esp. p. 330.

structuralists put it so well. There are no examples of a language without an entire area untranslatable. Everything we know has a signification, a meaning that is always incarnated in a system, our universe of language. As soon as a language 'exists', it is the universe'.[24]

My wish here is not particularly to examine the specific word 'certainty' or '*sécurité*' in the particular universe constituted by the English or the French languages.[25] Rather, it should be about another question that Oedipus might have asked the Sphinx: when we are talking and writing on 'certainty' or '*sécurité*' in a comparative work, are we talking and/or writing on/of the same 'thing'? We should carefully consider the point of irreducible impossibility to reconcile meanings of that same 'thing', together with the postulate that comparing starts with respecting the others, their laws, and therefore the differences of the others rather than the similarities of the others. In fact, even if we were certain that the words certainty or *sécurité* had the same meaning in French and in English, we should not start from this hypothesis, but on the contrary, critically think, i.e. decide that we cannot be entirely certain that 'certainty' has the same meaning as '*sécurité*'. In consequence, we are obviously obliged to rely on approximation based on the assumption that we have a 'good', a 'right' or 'truthful' translation, in both direction, but keeping in mind, a critical mind, that it may not be the case. We have to imagine, in a way, a certain idea of what the discourse of the other, across the Channel is, or even should be, like a perception of that discourse. Perhaps we should turn to scholars such as Dicey, Austin and Hart, in order to grasp and expose the English or British *mentalité*,[26] pointing out here what Heidegger states in his *Introduction a la Métaphysique*[27]: 'Cette traduction (ici du grec en romain) n'est pas indifférente ni anodine, c'est au contraire la premiere étape d'un processus de fermeture et d'aliénation (...)' and:

> 'il s'agit maintenant pour nous de sauter par dessus ce processus de déformation et de dégradation, et de chercher a reconquérir la force d'appellation intacte de la langue et des mots; car ces mots et la langue ne sont pas de petits sachets dans lesquels les choses seraient simplement enveloppées pour le trafic des paroles et de l'écrits.'[28]

This is what is at stake here. Alienation of meanings. In the comparison of the signifier and the signified of the words 'certainty' or '*sécurité*' in a comparative perspective, there is a deformation, a degradation, and ultimately we cannot have purity in the translation. But that is not an issue because we can just keep in mind the impossible reconciliation,

24 Ibid., p. 331.

25 I will do so both as a distant expert and a *candide*. A distant expert living for year now in common law countries, a *candide* working on comparative law and linguistic.

26 Dicey, AV, *Introduction to the Law of the Constitution*, London McMillan 8th ed. 1927. Note that Dicey formalise for example the 'position' of the parliament in the English Constitution by exposing the common law understanding of the law maker: "... Parliament thus defined (i.e., the Queen in Parliament) has under the English constitution the right to make or unmake any law whatever; and further that no person or body is recognised by the law of England as having a right to override or set aside the legislation of Parliament".

27 Heidegger, M., *Introduction a la Métaphysique*, Gallimard TEL, 1967, esp. p. 26.

28 Ibid., esp. p. 26.

which should to some extend suffice to protect our intellectual process. What is perhaps tricky at that stage is to keep in mind the history of England and particularly the Norman Conquest.[29] The Norman brought in England, among other elements, a language, that will become the legal language of England and the common law. This is confirmed by Legrand and Samuel, who noted that in fact that is the French language that was brought in. Indeed, the French language was used for the common law until very recently. It was gradually replaced by English, the British parliament replacing it in its procedure, only in the 18th century. Even though, the 'English' used in law was always said to be 'Law French'.[30] That is a clear evidence that the English legal terminology was strongly penetrated by the French equivalent. The importance of the French language in legal vocabulary of the common law obliges us to consider therefore first and foremost Latin, one of the source of the French language, Roman law, being of course one of the basis of legal French itself. One of the most authoritative Latin-French dictionary, the 'Gaffiot,' should constitute here not only an accurate record of the origin of the words used but also ultimately a demonstration of the process of its penetration in the English language.

Certainty for instance, suggests a firm, settled belief or positiveness in the truth of something. *Sécurité* would suggest absence of worries, of feelings related to danger.

Certainty came into Middle English as certainte or certeinte and derives from the Old French word *certaineté* (certitude, assuré). It refers originally to a pledge or surety, that we could relate somehow to *sécurité*. *Sécurité* originates from *securitas*, which translate not only as *sécurité* as *tranquilité* of the soul but also as *sûreté*. Certainty is primarily the quality of being certain, the French equivalent of reliable or sure. The Latin *certus*, origin of certain, confirms the idea of sure, fixed, settled, determined.

According to the *Theory of Legal Certainty* of John Braithwaite, certainty, consistency and reliability may be used interchangeably for certainty. He defines a theoretical framework for legal certainty built around terminology.[31]

1. When the type of action to be regulated is simple, stable (not changing unpredictably across time) and does not involve huge economic interests, rules regulate with greater certainty than principles.
2. With complex actions in changing environments where large economic interests are at stake principles are more likely to enable legal certainty than rules.[32]

4. For Gutteridge, increase collaboration between English and foreign jurists was the key of the success of comparative law.[33] Ideally, a comparatist should be opened to the law of the other, to this other law, to become this other. Comparative law appears to be the promise of an encounter, the encounter of the other. We may decide that the best way

29 Legrand, P. & Samuel, G., *Introduction au common law*, Paris Reperes, 2008, pp. 25–26.

30 Ibid., pp. 23–24.

31 Braithwaite, J., 'Rules and Principles: A Theory of Legal Certainty', 27 *Australian Journal of Legal Philosophy* 47, 2002, pp. 1–46, esp. p. 4.

32 Ibid, p. 37.

33 Gutteridge, H.C., 'The Study of Comparative Law in France and England', 4 *J. Comp. Legis. & Int'l L.* 3d, 1922, pp. 82–88, esp. p. 88.

to compare for the jurist is actually to dive into interdisciplinary work. This other becomes then the other discipline.

> Arguments for interdisciplinarity generally stem from debates surrounding disciplinarity. Within arguments for interdisciplinarity, two main threads can be found. The first argues for interdisciplinarity normatively, positioning it either in terms of filling the gaps that disciplinarity leaves vacant or in terms of transcendence surpassing what disciplinarity can ever hope to achieve.[34]

Inter disciplinarity should therefore be understood as filling gaps that the specialisation cannot fill but also going further than that specialisation. That is not very far from the gap that is filled by comparative law, bridge between cultures and traditions. Adding comparative legal research to economics is a step further that can only help to fill gaps that both disciplines are facing.

> Besides the normative arguments, the second type of argument for interdisciplinarity is more phenomenological in the sense that it emanates from observations of practice. This view posits that interdisciplinarity already exists within disciplines. The organisation of disciplinarity and interdisciplinarity is intertwined historically, with interdisciplinarity (most often) quietly flourishing within disciplines.[35]

Interdisciplinarity, as a result, should be quite a 'normal' exercise. In fact, law and economics are never very far, lawyers including comparative lawyers, work with economics, sometimes without knowing it, while economists cannot really study in their field without considering the legal framework surrounding them. And what to say about a Marxist analysis of the law ... This is true particularly when a research project aims to link more than one jurisdictions. According to Dau-Schmidt, there are three ways that two disciplines can relate to each other: free and open communication over shared problems for the benefit of both disciplines; indifference with segregated subject matter; open hostility or 'imperialism', with one or both disciplines vying to take over the other's subject matter and/or means of analysis.[36] Moving from working in one discipline to many disciplines can bring dilemmas ranging from very optimistic approach to very pessimistic approach. Again, this is not very different from the challenges facing the work of comparison in the legal field. It is particularly useful to learn that 'The prospects for a useful interdisciplinary exchange between economics and sociology on law seem particularly bright'.[37]

34 Chettiparamb, A., 'Interdisciplinarity: a literature review', *The Interdisciplinary Teaching and Learning Group, Subject Centre for Languages, Linguistics and Area Studies*, School of Humanities, University of Southampton, 2007, pp. 1–46, esp. p. 13.

35 Ibid., p. 15.

36 Dau-Schmidt, Kenneth G., 'Economics and Sociology: The Prospects for an Interdisciplinary Discourse on Law', *Wis. L. Rev.* (1997), pp. 389–420, esp. p. 391.

37 Ibid., esp. p. 406.

> 'Recent work in economics and sociology shows substantial overlap in methodology and examined subject matter and thus the potential for useful exchange. The potential for useful exchange seems particularly strong with respect to subjects, such as law, which are not the traditional domain of economics and which may not always be well-explained by the traditional neoclassical economic model.[38]

In the analysis of law, the work of sociologists may be useful in suggesting ways in which the assumptions of the traditional economic model should be relaxed in order to produce superior predictive and explanatory models. At least three such implications of sociology for the economic analysis of law seem readily apparent. First, it would seem important to take account of the fact that people are not always independent actors, but are members of groups, and that such membership can sometimes affect their actions. (...). Second, people are inculcated with certain norms of cooperation, and these norms sometimes dictate actions that are not purely self-interested. The acknowledgement of such norms for cooperation may be important in the analysis of a wide variety of legal issues (...). Finally, it is important to take account of the fact that the law is not merely a pricing mechanism, but is sometimes intended to "socialize" people and influence their preferences with respect to a particular activity.'[39]

To sum up these too brief remarks on comparison in law and inter disciplinarity, we should remember that primarily comparing law is a difficult exercise of the mind that is built on the core on the self in its social, inter-personal, dimension. It can be done via many methods but always with the respect of the other/s studied. It is an exercise that builds on law, sociology, and linguistic. Comparing law seems to be an interdisciplinary work that fits well with a project that is not only between 'national' things but also interdisciplinary. According to Dau-Schmidt, the inter disciplinary discourse of the law is a discourse of sociology. Through this apparent or even evident assumption, we can only deduct that a socio-legal approach has to be adopted because it can be deemed as satisfactory for both law, and particularly comparative law, and economics, in an inter disciplinary work.

38 Ibid., esp. p. 418.
39 Ibid., esp. p. 419.

PART I

THE IDEA OF LEGAL CERTAINTY

A. Theoretical Approach

Régis Lanneau*

WHAT IS LEGAL CERTAINTY? A THEORETICAL ESSAY

"From time to time it is probably necessary to detach oneself from the technicalities of the argument and to ask quite naively what it is all about"[1]
Friedrich Hayek

Many legal concepts seem to be perfectly clear to neophytes but in fact prove to be highly complex when it comes to determining if not their meaning, then at least their gist. Legal certainty definitely belongs to this category. As for beauty or democracy, it is possible to sense its meaning without being able to explain it clearly.

It formed part of the collective legal unconscious for many years until it was given a firm legal basis in case law by the ECJ in 1962 (*SNUPAT*[2] and *Bosch*[3] judgements) and then by the ECHR in 1979 (*Marckx* judgement[4]). It was not incorporated into the French legal grammar until 2006 via the KPMG[5] judgement made by the *Conseil d'Etat* (Council of State). Since then, post-rationalisations have led to its recognition in the French Declaration of the Rights of Man and of the Citizen (in a clever combination of articles 2 and 7 – on certainty – and 16 – on the guarantee of rights), as an implicit constitutional

* Professor (Maitre de conférences) in Public Law at the Université de Paris Ouest Nanterre La Défense, CRDP, FIDES.

1 Friedrich Hayek, *Economics and Knowledge*, 1937, *Economica*, London, vol IV, pp 33–54, p 54; reproduced in Friedrich Hayek, *Individualism and Economic Order*, [1948] 1992, Chicago University Press, Chicago, 272 pages, pp 33–56, p 56.

2 ECJ, *SNUPAT v. High Authority*, 22 March 1961, Joined cases C-42 and 49/59.

3 ECJ, *Kledingverkoopbedrijf de Geus en Uitdenbogerd versus Robert Bosch GmbH and Maatschappij tot voortzetting van de zaken der Firma Willem van Rijn*, 14 July 1972, aff. 57/69; also see ECJ, 14 July 1972, *Azienda Colori Nazionali v. Commission*, aff. 57–69.

4 ECHR, *Marckx v. Belgium*, 13 June 1979, series A no 31, pp. 14–15.

5 CE, *KPMG company et al.*, ass, 24 March 2006, "Considering that in addition to compliance with this requirement, it is incumbent upon the authority invested with regulatory power to enact, for reasons of legal certainty, the transitional measures required, if applicable, by a new regulation."

"value"[6], or indeed as the basis of the rule of law.[7] As for any new concept, it has led to new readings and new ways of structuring the law, which seems to be unaware of its constitution.

This late appearance of the concept in legal history could be explained by the Tocqueville effect.[8] When a particular phenomenon declines, any reappearances of this phenomenon become increasingly intolerable. The concept of legal certainty may thus have appeared at this precise moment in history in which legal certainty is already very prevalent within modern legal systems and, in a certain sense, no longer poses problems, becoming established as an implicit requirement of a "good" legal system.

Without really seeking to theorise this notion, law, case law and their reinterpretation by the doctrine, have caused legal certainty to become a "global concept"[9] – a concept defined by a sum of components whose completeness is never postulated: non-retroactivity[10], accessibility and intelligibility[11], normativity and quality of the law[12], consistency of the law and case law[13], and the need for transitional measures in order to cope with an instability or unpredictability of the law[14], etc. However, the way in which case law operates leads to a negative affirmation of the notion: it does not say what legal certainty actually is but rather what it is not. This approach never allows a debate to be "closed"; on the contrary it means it is always left open.

While the concept of legal certainty unifies these different components – at least in theory – what creates the unity of the global concept still needs to be defined or, more precisely, is only rarely explained. If the jurist is merely seeking to identify what has been

6 Which did not prevent the *Conseil constitutionnel* (Constitutional Council) from refusing to recognise this principle in 1984 (84–184 DC of 29 December 1984) before constitutionalising its "substance" progressively (the term clearly appears in the judgement 2007–547 DC of 15 February 2007). For example, see Bertrand Mathieu, "La sécurité juridique, un principe clandestin mais efficient", in *Mélanges Patrice Gélard*, 2000, Montchrestien, Paris, 490 pp, particularly p 301. In this article, however, the concept of legal certainty is not described in detail, just some of its "components" play a central role in the reasoning.

7 "The principle of legal certainty seems to be the last rampart of supreme courts wishing to maintain some semblance of order and to allow law to fulfil its normal function" Olivier Dutheillet de Lamothe, Franco-Brazilian seminar, Court of Cassation, 19 September 2005.

8 "The pain that used to be tolerated patiently on the grounds that it was inevitable suddenly seems to be intolerable once the decision has been made to escape from it. Anything that we thus subtract from the abuses only seems to magnify what remains and makes the suffering even more intense: the pain is certainly diminished but the sensitivity has increased" Tocqueville, L'Ancien Régime et la Révolution, [1856], in Tocqueville, Œuvres, vol 3, 2004, Bibliothèque de la Pléiade, Paris, pp 41–451, p 202.

9 Or even a "multipurpose concept", Pierre Pescatore, *Les principes généraux communs aux droits des Etats Membres en tant que source du droit communautaire*, Report of the 12th FIDE Congress, 1986, Volume 1, Paris, 24–27 September 1986, p 33.

10 Established by both the French Civil Code (*Code civil* – article 2) and by administrative case law (CE, *Société du journal L'Aurore*, 25 June 1948). To quote Portalis, "The function of the law is to sort out the future; it no longer has any power over the past. Wherever retroactivity is permitted, certainty no longer exists and nor does even a shadow of it" (Portalis, Preliminary speech for the first draft of the Code civil, 1801).

11 *Conseil Constitutionnel* (Constitutional Council), no. 99–421 DC of 16 December 1999.

12 *Conseil Constitutionnel* (Constitutional Council), no. 2005–512 DC of 21 April 2005. The Constitutional Council states that the rules must also be precise and unequivocal.

13 This is required in order to offer the possibility of understanding the law.

14 CE, *KPMG company et al.*, ass, 24 March 2006.

positively identified by the idea of legal certainty, this cataloguing is certainly useful, but if the aim is to build consistency into the legal grammar, it would be absurd to remain at this level. After all, the idea of legal certainty may concern the legal concept of legal certainty and law can no longer be simply designed from within due to the self-reference effect. It is consequently a question of stepping outside the legal field in an attempt to create a rationale for it (which is only legal in terms of its purpose).

It thus proves necessary to theorise the notion. What could be its rationale? What could be its dimensions?[15]

The majority of works on legal certainty only address these issues in a peripheral manner: they either involve specifying the case law or developing an analogous topic. The question of the meaning at the "meta" level, as a concept concerning law rather than a legal concept, is rarely envisaged, to the extent that the function of legal certainty is insufficiently understood. Indeed, legal certainty, as it appears in the doctrine or case law, is no more than a return to a conception of the rule of law. This reading backs up the idea of the Tocqueville effect: legal certainty is only a problem in a well established rule of law and is ultimately just a return to this notion. This point can be clearly revealed in Lon Fuller's and, to a lesser extent, in Hayek's analyses.[16] The function of legal certainty can be reduced to the function of the rule of law (I). The theorising with regard to function of legal certainty is therefore complete. However, its different dimensions have been rarely considered and there is no doubt that they can shed light on the problem of legal certainty (II).

1. The function of legal certainty: identical to the function of the rule of law

Legal certainty is often considered to be a characteristic of a good law. It is rather surprising that no link has yet been made in order to differentiate between legal certainty and the rule of law. From a functional standpoint, these two notions are identical so that the analyses and remarks made prior to the appearance of the concept allow for a reinterpretation of the current debates by putting them into context. The characteristics of legal certainty correspond quite consistently to the characteristics identified by Lon Fuller with regard to the rule of law (A)... and even to the abstraction of the meaning of each of these characteristics. However, the jusnaturalist dimension must be eliminated from its conception so that it can correspond to its current uses... even if this dimension relates to the system more than to individual rights. This link also reveals an obvious fact: legal certainty is not completely unrelated to a "moral" conception of the law (the relationship in this case is holistic). Similarly, the Hayekian approach stresses the idea of protecting legitimate expectations, which to some extent echoes the idea of legitimate expectations (B). This distinction also helps us to understand a linguistic difference between "legal certainty" and "legitimate expectations". The former remains rooted in a conception of the law that could almost be self-justifying. It is the characteristic of a good law and a

15 This is a question of proposing one possible interpretation of legal certainty. It is obviously not the only one possible.

16 This choice could have been different and many aspects of Hayek's analysis are proposed elsewhere, particularly by Montesquieu.

means by which the law "operates" properly. The latter instrumentalises the notion to a greater extent. Legal certainty is only pertinent to the extent that its economic effects are taken into account.

1.1. Legal certainty: a condition for an efficient incentive system – a reinterpretation of Lon Fuller

Lon Fuller, in his book *Law and Morality*[17], expounds on the parable of King Rex. Having recently come to power, King Rex wishes to improve his country's legal system and to this end, he implements reforms. The whole point of the fable is to identify eight parameters of a "good" legal system, which are not unlike the components of legal certainty identified by both the doctrine and case law: intelligibility, limited variability, accessibility, non-retroactivity of the law, etc. This reinterpretation has already been proposed by Hart.[18]

For Lon Fuller, it is a question of envisaging the characteristics of a good law without looking further into the economic impact of such a situation or the concept of legal certainty. He elaborates on the reasons by which the "rule of law" can be maintained. By reinterpreting his thinking, he identifies the characteristics of an effective and efficient incentive system.

Rex, discovering that establishing general laws is a difficult undertaking, decides to settle disputes on a case-by-case basis only. In such a system, there are only specific rules and the law cannot act as a coordinator of individual citizens' actions. For the system to fail to create legal certainty, there must also be no rules enshrining respect for precedents or the consistency of judgements. In any case, legal certainty is not a characteristic of such a system from the outset.

The failure of this initial reform thus forces the king to make general laws, but he refuses to have them published. Although Rex then strives to enforce the rules that he has laid down, the population is not aware of them. Therefore, it cannot «count on» them to govern its choices of actions. Once again, legal certainty is far from ensured, precisely because the rules cannot be known, apart from through experience, which implies that the rules are invariable, and this is not necessarily the case.

Rex realises that their non-publication is a failure. He thus decides to wait until the end of each year to judge the cases brought to him before publishing the rules that he had applied in order to settle these cases. This raises the problem of retroactivity. None of the laws are published before their application. Individuals cannot rely on the law to guide their choices of actions.

So Rex decides to publish a code in response to the disputes. However, the articles of this code and the links between them are difficult to establish. The rules lack clarity and may even be described as unintelligible. In this case, the citizens are given a code which provides the "rules", but as they are incomprehensible, they cannot be used to change their behaviour or increase legal certainty.

17 Lon Fuller, *The Morality of Law*, 1964, Yale University Press, New Haven, 262 pp.

18 "to call the principles of the poisoner's art "the morality of poisoning" would simply blur the distinction between the notion of efficiency for a purpose and those final judgments about activities and purposes with which morality in its various forms is concerned" H.L.A. Hart, Book Review, 1965, *Harvard Law Review*, vol 78, pp 1281–1296, especially p 1286.

As King Rex's code is criticised, the good king decides to rewrite it in order to improve its clarity. Unfortunately, the rewritten code proves to be hugely inconsistent: there is not a single provision that is not contradicted by a different provision. The vagueness of the rules cancels out any incentive effects of the laws.

Confronted with renewed criticisms, Rex's irritation boils over. He therefore decides to rid the code of its contradictions, but the rules now impose behaviours which are impossible for his subjects to emulate. They know what they are supposed to do but they are unable to put them into practice. So what is the point of the laws? In this case, there is no legal certainty due to it being impossible for the citizens to adopt a "legal" position.

The magnanimous King Rex then decides to enlist expert help and strives creating the best possible code. As the road to hell is paved with good intentions, his obsession with perfection drives him to modify the code as soon as it is published. The law is constantly evolving and there is no guarantee that a rule laid down yesterday will not be changed tomorrow. Without any doubt, the degree of variability of the law is also a parameter of legal certainty.

Finally, Rex wonders whether he could reduce this variability by settling disputes himself by using or not using the code as he sees fit. In this case, nothing guarantees that the law will be applied by the State with the result that the "legal" positions remain unstable.

For all that, Lon Fuller's approach is not a theorisation of the concept of legal certainty or of the "rule of law". While he certainly identifies components of it, he does not explain the reasons for the structure of his reasoning. It has to be acknowledged that the doctrine and case law have not gone any further. Legal certainty is a list of components whose unity should seem so obvious that there is no point in specifying it.

In addition, Lon Fuller identifies the "problems" encountered by King Rex without envisaging possible trade-offs between the cost of resolving these problems and the gains in terms of the "quality" of the law. However, it was only possible to develop this subject by further instrumentalising the legal system and therefore the concept of legal certainty.

1.2. *Legal certainty: a requirement for an efficient coordination of individuals, Hayekian intuitions*

In contrast to Lon Fuller, Hayek is more explicit concerning the function of the rules of law: "*The aim of rules must be to facilitate that matching or tallying of the expectations on which the plans of the individuals depend for their success*".[19] Legal certainty is thus interpreted as the principle of legitimate expectations; the meaning of these two concepts is less divergent than the emphasis that is placed on their instrumentality. The reasoning proposed by the professor of economics thus illustrates a possible rationale for legal certainty that is rarely put forward.

For Hayek, the fundamental problem of society is the effective and efficient coordination of individuals. If the rationality of these people is limited, the action is thus primarily based on suppositions. Laws intervene at this level. By formulating rules they provide collective points of reference for individuals, which facilitate coordination to a great extent.

19 F.A. Hayek, *Droit, Législation et Liberté tome 1*, [1973] 1995, PUF, Quadrige, Vendôme, 208 pp., p 117.

Society is a complex phenomenon and it would be absurd to seek maximum certainty for all expectations. Only legitimate expectations shall receive (and for Hayek must receive) government protection. Ensuring the certainty of legitimate expectations allows society to exist, but too much inflexibility prevents society from evolving. The idea of legitimacy reveals the balance between these two constraints. In other words, it would be absurd and even impossible for laws to provide certainty for all expectations.

The rules must allow individuals to know how the State will use its powers of coercion, which means that they must be aware of them before they are applied[20] This is a fundamental attribute of the rules: "*there is probably no single factor which has contributed more to the prosperity of the West than the relative certainty of the law which has prevailed here*".[21] This encapsulates the idea of publication and also the idea of the intelligibility of the law (often presumed by Hayek).

Rules of law endowed with relative certainty improve the anticipation of the agents and therefore lead to better overall coordination and a faster response in terms of adjustments. "*The rules merely provide the framework within which the individual must move but within which the decisions are his*".[22] This need for coordination and certainty means that the rules must not be contradictory. Moreover, this final criterion is crucial for his "test" of justice: "*The test is thus in the last resort, one of the compatibility or non contradictoriness of the whole system of rules, not merely in a logical sense but in the sense that the system of actions which the rules permit will not lead to conflict*".[23]

Legal certainty could be measured by the lack of legal proceedings. Effective laws are those whose fundamentals can be renegotiated – this bears a resemblance to the Coase approach. Uncertainty about the law inevitably heralds its decline, as individuals can no longer rely on it to coordinate their actions. For Hayek, the certainty of laws does not in any way originate from their formulation – he believes that laws are discovered more than they are created – due to the limitations of language.[24] This does not mean that the formulation of a rule is irrelevant, but that any formulation is bound to be imperfect as it reflects "principles" that individuals must be able to "sense" via written rules or case law.

The Hayekian approach very clearly exploits the concept of legal certainty without really modifying its components. As the value of legal certainty is not assessed in itself, it is possible to define fundamental trade-offs (e.g. between inflexibility and evolution and more broadly between the costs and benefits of legal certainty). These trade-offs are not considered in Lon Fuller's approach.

20 F.A. Hayek, *The Road to Serfdom*, [1944] 1994, Chicago University Press, Chicago, 274 pp, pp. 80–81.

21 F.A. Hayek, *The Constitution of Liberty*, [1960] 1992, Chicago University Press, Chicago, 568 pp., p 208.

22 F.A. Hayek, *The Constitution of Liberty*, op cit, p 152. also see F.A. Hayek, *The Road to Serfdom*, op cit, pp. 81, 82: Hayek makes a distinction between "formal laws" and "substantive rules".

23 F.A. Hayek, *Principles of a Liberal Social Order*, in F.A. *Hayek, Studies in Philosophy, Politics and Economics*, 1967, Routledge and Kegan Paul, London, 356 pp, pp. 160–177, p 168. It should be noted that he criticises the purely formal approach to law in general. This point is found, for example, in F.A. Hayek, *The Constitution of Liberty*, op cit, p 238.

24 F.A. Hayek, *Droit, Législation et Liberté, tome 1*, op cit, p 105, for example.

However, legal certainty is not a requirement of law insofar as it is not used to define law as a right. It is instrumentally perceived as a requirement for "good" law. However, the general function does not allow us to enter fully into the heart of the concept.

2. The three dimensions of legal certainty

Once the functions and rationale of legal certainty have been identified, we can then attempt to conceptualise its dimensions. This conceptualisation does not seek to set anything in stone but to provide a global approach to considering legal certainty as both a theoretical item and a concept of case law. It also allows for the identification of the dimensions of legal certainty that have not yet been mobilised by case law but which could quite easily be.

As legal certainty is dependent on the link between fact and law, three dimensions may appear.[25] Firstly, there is certainty concerning the content of the laws themselves, i.e. material legal certainty (A). Secondly, there is certainty concerning the transition from fact into law – in other words, procedural legal certainty (B). Finally, there is certainty which, in forming a loop, links law to the fact – a form of certainty in the efficacy of law (C).

These different dimensions of legal certainty may reflect the characteristics of an entire legal system (e.g. the French legal system), or of some of its subsets (e.g. administrative law, civil law or contract law). It thus implies the definition of a "field" so that it can be assessed.

Figure 1 shows a graphical representation of the analysis grid (at the synchronic level)

Figure 1

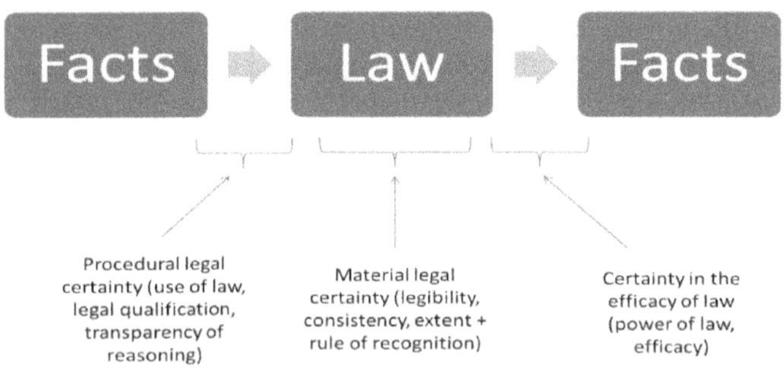

Legal certainty does not appear as an "objective" notion; it depends on an expectation – or even a feeling – of the stakeholders and can even be considered to be purely conventional (see below). This notion is consequently applied in a diachronic approach. The distinctions made subsequently shall not seek to achieve an "objective" assessment, but shall instead seek fields of subjective assessment of the degree of legal certainty that develops with the "looping" and repetition of patterns on the subject. This idea of looping can justify the inclusion of the concept in the context of the Tocqueville effect. The acceptability

25 Peczenik distinguishes between formal legal certainty (predictability) and substantive certainty (acceptability) (Aleksander Peczenik, *On Law and Reason*, 1989, Kluwer Academic Publishers, London, 364 pp., pp 24–33.

threshold of legal uncertainty is thus variable.[26] Likewise, as the notion is subjective, there is nothing to prevent distinctions from being made between the legal certainty perceived by one type of stakeholders and that perceived by another type of stakeholders. In other words, "acceptable" legal certainty may depend on a relationship that is maintained with the law. A judge, a lawyer an academic and an ordinary citizen might not have the same perception of the level attained by each dimension of legal certainty.

Figure 2 schematically illustrates the idea of diachronic legal certainty and identifies the existing loops. These loops simply show the learning mechanism that operates for stakeholders in the legal system.

Figure 2

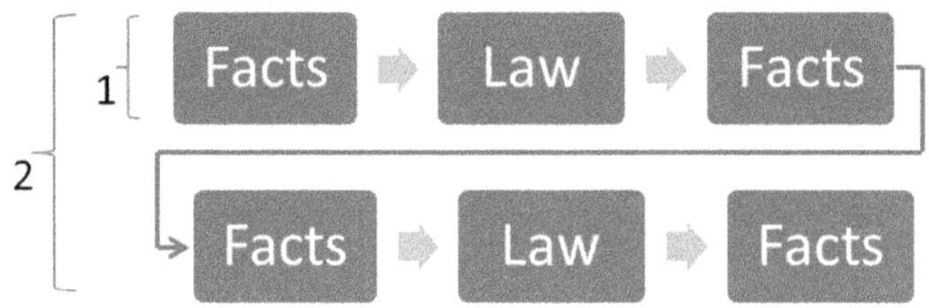

1: synchronic dimension
2: diachronic dimension

It may also be possible to add a legal meta-certainty, i.e. a legal certainty concerning the level of legal certainty in a system, but this would have little impact on the analysis (it would just be a question of transposing the concepts developed to the meta level).

There cannot be complete legal certainty throughout each of its dimensions for the reasons put forward by Hayek; the law must be able to evolve. Consequently, legal certainty is not an objective quality but a conventional or "inter-subjective" judgement. Therefore, legal certainty does not impose a mechanical type of law – a legal mathematics covering both syntax and semantics; it is more concerned with a procedural dimension.

It should be remembered that this is a question of legal certainty, which is not a "factual" type of certainty. Even if the laws are not efficient, or are unstable, factual certainty may exist if other normative systems take over from the "official" laws. Factual certainty may be ensured by law and, in principle, is supposed to be less "costly". Economic agents are more interested in seeking factual certainty than legal certainty.

2.1. Material legal certainty

A rigorous approach requires a distinction to be made between synchronic and diachronic aspects of material legal certainty.

26 And it is not necessarily in just one direction. It is likely that trade-offs are made between the different dimensions of legal certainty.

1. *Synchronic material legal certainty* assesses the degree of legal certainty in the legal grammar at a given moment. The legal grammar defines the conditions for the formulation of "correct" legal statements.

a. On an initial level, legal certainty thus concerns the grammar being sufficiently *intelligible*. This intelligibility seeks to facilitate the identification of links between the legal categories (the public service category is linked to the public interest category, the government control category, the prerogative of public power category and each of the categories is linked to other categories) and semantic intelligibility (the appearance of meaning in the legal field, even though the meaning of law has less to do with synchronic material legal certainty than with procedural legal certainty. The latter may indeed distinguish between language and legal language[27]). It also – and above all – implies the accessibility of law, and without this factor, any law is necessarily less intelligible.

b. For this grammar to be sufficiently intelligible, it needs to be *consistent*.[28] In other words, the legal categories must be in logical or almost logical relationships (it should be possible to create a mathematics of the concepts, as idealised by Pandectism, but at a semantic level, which explains its failure; by remaining at the syntactic level, the pitfalls can be avoided. At this level, this condition does not need to concern the relationship between the meaning of the categories – since it concerns grammar and semantics.

c. Finally, the grammar must ideally *specify its scope*. It must allow for the identification of what relates to law and what does not. To this end, we must make a change from simple syntactic formation without becoming bogged down in semantics. This is an intermediate level. The scope of the grammar also depends on the procedural dimension, but even without case law, it should be possible to determine its approximate limits. This dimension also supposes an ability to identify what law actually is (Hart's "rule of recognition"[29])

2. *Diachronic legal certainty* raises the question of the stability of grammar – in other words, of the *variability of content or of the relationships between the legal categories*. This variability concerns the relationships between the legal categories identified in the texts and the grammatical contribution of case law[30]; this is an indication of the stability of

27 Without pre-empting, one only has to think about the link between the public interest and "gambling", which is only meaningful in the legal domain. It should also be mentioned that a legal word may "vary" or at least be "adapted" to the circumstances. It is thus unlikely that the Constitution of the United States has the same meaning today as it had two centuries ago, while the words remain unchanged.

28 It should be noted that the doctrine frequently assumes the existence of this consistency but then goes on to reformulate it or define its meaning… one only has to think back to the debates about the criterion of administrative law at the start of the 20th century.

29 H.L.A. Hart, *The Concept of Law*, 2nd Edition, 1967, Clarendon Law Series, Oxford, 315 pp.

30 For example, in administrative law, the APREI order (CE, sect., 22 January 2007) adds to the famous *Narcy* case law (CE, sect., 28 June 1953) by stating that "*even in the absence of such prerogatives [of public power], a private person must also be regarded, in the absence of legal provisions, as carrying out a public service mission when, in view of the public interest of his or her activity, the conditions of its creation, organisation or operation, the obligations imposed upon him or her and the measures implemented in*

the law over time. It covers the three dimensions identified for synchronic material legal certainty. The greater the assurance of this certainty, the more rigid is the law. The problem of identifying an appropriate level of diachronic material legal certainty is then raised.

This diachronic material certainty also concerns the question of *retroactivity*. While a variation in the grammar might be understandable for the future, doing so for the past would amount to depriving synchronic material legal certainty of its substance: certainty cannot be guaranteed at the synchronic level if retroactivity is a possibility (from this standpoint, the retroactivity of case law is certainly a heresy[31]). Because of this dimension, transitional measures may be implemented by judges (these measures signify that the legal grammar could be too severely impacted; a balance is directly sought between inflexibility and change).[32]

This distinction does not mean that the concepts are watertight. It is thus possible for the law to specify the limits of variability of the grammar at a given moment, which will influence diachronic material legal certainty.

Finally, the meta level cannot be excluded. Legal certainty at the meta level targets the degree of confidence in the anticipation of the variability that is possible in both dimensions of material legal certainty.

2.2. *Procedural legal certainty*

Procedural legal certainty concerns the use that judges make of legal grammar (including that which they help to create). This legal certainty also concerns two levels.

1. Synchronic procedural legal certainty corresponds to an indication of confidence relating to the methods of reasoning used by judges that may extend to the perfect predictability of their judgements.[33] This supposes that the judges are not machines of random production. Three levels are concerned.

order to check on the achievement of the assigned objectives, it appears that the administration had intended to entrust such a mission to him or her". This is merely a "grammatical" addition insofar as a new line of justification is now open. Diachronic material certainty may also concern the meaning of categories. The Koné order (CE, ass., 3 juillet 1996) could also be mentioned, in which the Conseil d'Etat *(Council of State) independently creates or discovers a fundamental principle recognised by the laws of the French Republic.*

31 For example, see CE, *SCI Saint Lazare*, 14 June 2004; CE, *Louis*, 28 September 2005.

32 The typical example is certainly the Tropic Travaux Signalisation company order of 16 July 2007: "that however, with regard to the necessity for legal certainty requiring that current contractual relationships are not adversely affected, and subject to legal proceedings with the same purpose and which have already been undertaken prior to the date of the reading of this judgement, the action defined hereinabove can only be instigated against contracts whose execution procedure was begun after this date".

33 Seeing the capacity to predict that resides in legal certainty hides the real reasons for this possibility, i.e. the knowledge of procedures and modes of reasoning used by judges.

It may firstly relate to the *place of the announced law in the judges' reasoning*. This level of legal certainty is relatively easy to achieve and means that the judges are using the announced law, even if they do not make exclusive use of it. Substantive law (law and case law) must be included in their reasoning[34] and there must be sufficient compliance with its grammar.[35]

It is then concerned with the *legal qualification of facts*. This involves verifying that the judge conforms to the conventions of a language and that he or she is consistent in the transition from the real world to the legal world (even if the legal world contributes to the creation of the real world).[36] The law settles for specifying the legal categories and their relationships. It is a language, but one whose creation is based on a "natural" language. Ideally, the legal qualification should closely conform to the conventions of natural language. It may also conform to the legal language conventions created by repetition and professional deformation associated with the learning of law. This implies consistency in the reasoning and very directly concerns the predictability of law (this predictability does not imply strict compliance with the texts but rather a consistency in the judges' reasoning; case law regains its primary status). At this level, it is possible to consider the degree of legal certainty about the case-law definition of legal certainty.

Finally, it more deeply concerns the judge's reasoning and therefore the *transparency of this reasoning*. Insofar as case law contributes to the formation of law, it must comply with the conditions of material legal certainty – particularly the condition of intelligibility. It is certainly at this level that the jurisdictions of countries with civil law systems need to make the most "progress". Indeed, by presenting their solution as a logical one[37], or even as an authoritative solution, the crux of the reasoning is hidden from persons brought before the law or, to a lesser extent, is relegated to a position outside case law proper (e.g. in the conclusions of the *rapporteur public* [reporting judge]).[38] This knowledge may either be "abstract, i.e. relating to practical experience of non-formulatable law (principles), or more "concrete" when the legal possibilities are

34 Citations fulfil this very need, as does the use of laws, regulations or articles of code(s) in the text of a decision.

35 This compliance with grammar does not mean that it is impossible to develop it but on the contrary, it points to a reluctance to impoverish it.

36 From the "monumental perspective" or in the "general interest", does the judge have a conception of what constitutes a "meaning" for his or her audience? On this issue, it should be noted that legal qualifications are rarely the subject of debate in the text of a decision. This obviously influences the level of legal certainty as a whole.

37 Through the application of the famous syllogism… but also by refusing dissenting opinions.

38 For example, CE, *Commune de Dreux*, 13 May 1994 relating to the principle of equality before the public service. The judgement does not mention the issue of taxation, which is however clearly mentioned in the solicitor-general's findings. Moreover, on this subject, if the grammar of administrative law is summed up in the rendering of the orders of the *Conseil d'Etat* (Council of State), the meaning of "legal words" can only be understood on the basis of the findings of the *rapporteur public* (reporting judge). In one sense, these findings contribute to legal certainty… even if it is not compulsory for them to be published! In the case of the Constitutional Council's judgements, there is often mention of the importance of "authorised comments" whose legal significance is ranked below the judgement but above the mere doctrinal comment.

clearly presented. It may therefore mean a form of legal certainty relating to the outcome of the reasoning or a form of legal certainty relating to simple procedures, even though the outcome of the reasoning is not completely predictable (beyond a probabilistic approach).

In order to allow procedural certainty to include the reversals of case law, there must be a body of principles that make it possible to identify when such reversals may occur and have an impact. The technique used by the French *Conseil d'Etat* (Council of State) is often to carry out a reversal of case law in situations in which the application of the old or new rule makes no difference to the settlement of a specific case.[39] It should be noted that the reversal may concern either the grammar (modifying the relationships between categories), or the meaning of the categories with the grammar remaining constant.[40]

2. Diachronic procedural legal certainty concerns the possibility of varying the legal reasoning.

It includes the possibility of referring to past reasoning in order to anticipate the reasoning of the future. Even when case law is not the "source" of law, it provides approximations that it would be ridiculous to ignore.[41] Legal certainty requires only gradual changes in reasoning. The reasoning must remain stable for a certain period of time, even if some variability is acceptable when it can be anticipated.

Finally, it concerns mechanisms that allow for the limitation of this variability (e.g. two levels of judicial authority; sanctioning of judges; technique of transitional measures, etc.). It provides guarantees in the event of changes to reasoning by judges in such a way as to limit their effects, either by neutralising them (aborted attempt to reverse case law), by preventing them (modification that can be anticipated as it is announced[42]), or by approving new modes of reasoning while limiting their impact (technique of transitional measures).[43]

2.3. *Certainty in the efficacy of law*

Finally, legal certainty also concerns the efficacy of law. Even if the law is intelligible and the judge is not deemed to be eccentric, legal certainty still cannot be a factual reality. For it to become so, the court decisions need to be applied.

39 For example, the APREI order and the Nicolo order (CE, 20 October 1989). However, this is not always the case, as the Tropic order clearly shows... even though transitional measures were adopted in this case.

40 Paragraph 1 of article 1384, which was only meant to have been a little "scrap of an article", went on to become a major principle due to case law. Similarly, the notion of harm now concerns non-pecuniary loss, which has not always been recognised as a real form of harm.

41 The simple fact that the French Code civil (Civil Code) devotes more pages to case law than to articles reveals the importance of case law.

42 The doctrine considers certain types of case law to be "absurd", for example. From a more legal perspective, if we remain on the Tropic order, the European legal situation required such a change in case law; and what about the Perreux order (CE, ass., 30 October 2009) which is in keeping with the changes in case law, originating from the Cohn-Bendit order (CE, ass., 22 December 1978).

43 Still Tropic, or AC Association!

Legal certainty firstly concerns the *strength of the law*. If the law is not the most powerful normative system, it cannot guarantee factual certainty, which must be implemented according to the procedures of the most powerful normative system (effectively guaranteeing the coordination between individuals). For example, the maintenance of the caste system in India means that, on this issue, the law is not the most powerful normative system. The legal norms are not effective.

Legal power requires the law to be able to impose its authority against the other normative systems in the event of a conflict with them. Being supported by the law thus provides the very best level of certainty when this law is effective. In principle, this form of certainty is less costly (accessorily) than the provision of certainty by different means (e.g. by militia groups).

The law offers three types of techniques for protecting a situation, according to the typology applied by Calabresi and Melamed[44]: property rule, liability rule and inalienability. The property rule means that an individual cannot remove this right from its original "owner" without obtaining the latter's approval, generally after payment. The sanction is supposed to be severe enough to "impose" this prior negotiation. In the case of the property rule, it is possible to acquire the right without obtaining the holder's agreement by paying a certain price (here, the liability rule is conceptualised as a "call", i.e. an option to purchase for the person that does not possess the right). It is not the legal position that is made secure – only its value. The inalienability rule prohibits any exchange of rights.

These few clarifications of the notion of legal certainty help to reveal its close links to the idea of the rule of law, whether this is the desired goal in itself or a more instrumental dimension. They also provide a general typology that allows for the classification of case law judgements in a broader framework, thus assigning a unity to their content.

This unifying approach also helps to identify the trade-offs and therefore the elements that are not imposed by legal certainty. Legal certainty does not refer to the inflexibility of law but simply to its relatively large amount of predictability, which itself depends on a judgement. In this respect, legal certainty is therefore no different to legitimate expectations. If complete legal certainty leads to factual certainty, then the latter surpasses the strictly legal approach. Therefore, we must beware of confusing these two types of certainty. Finally, and in a traditional economic rationale, the costs and benefits of legal certainty must be counterbalanced, which seems to be carried out by case law, at least implicitly. Legal certainty can therefore only be understood in its practical dimension and examining it in relation to an unattainable ideal is bound to be unproductive. In other words, it cannot be positively defined – we can only sense its limits... and the typology proposed in the article sets out to improve this general integration of the notion of legal certainty.

44 Guido Calabresi and Douglas Melamed, Property Rules, Liability Rules, and Inalienability: One View of the Cathedral, 1972, *Harvard law Review*, vol 85, pp. 1089–1128.

B. Practical Approach

Youseph Farah

CONTRACTUAL CERTAINTY UNDER ENGLISH CONTRACT LAW

Legal certainty can influence the life of a bargain at a three crucial phases. These can be divided into pre-contractual, contractual and post-contractual. The logic behind this division in relation to legal certainty could partly be explained by understanding the emphasis that English contract law places on individual ethics, on the one hand and sanctity of agreements on the other. Thus the emphasis on bargaining [Atiyah] rather than on exchange of promises imposes a reading of the concept of legal certainty in that light. As a result pre-contractual negotiation may have little influence if any on the bargain, to some degree this fortified legal certainty rather than compromises it. on the other hand English doctrine of contract law would not concede except in exceptional circumstances to any variation to the bargain [unless freely undertaken, or agreed upon in the contract], nor a walk away from the bargain. The English court will not write a bargain for the parties, nor tolerate parties walking away from the bargain. There is a minimal role to substantive fairness or cooperative ethics in this phase. There is absoluteness to the bargain Parties are expected to comply with those obligation freely undertaken in the contract. Thus the contractual phase is also characterised by a great degree of certainty, possibly greater than the pre-contractual phase. Finally the pre-contractual phase, where one may argue that legal certainty will depend on the conduct and behaviour of the parties. On the one hand parties are expected to uphold a certain standard, for example mitigate a loss, or would be substituted by the reasonable man, taking into account principles common to open and fair dealing, and the principle of proportionality, which would affect the expected bargain [limits to the expectation interest- See Ruxely electronics]

1. Theory of English Contract law that shapes legal certainty

The ethos of English contract law can be best described as 'essentially individualistic' (Brownsword). The corner stone of that nature of English contract law are none other than the principles of freedom of contract, and the sanctity of agreements. This notion has survived despite the resurrection of welfarism ethics into English Contract law, and insofar as parties enter into binding agreements, under a 19th-century paradigm conforming to a carefully delineated doctrinal application, i.e. offer, acceptance, consideration, etc... The parties must agree on all the essential terms of the contract in order to have a binding agreement. Where agreements are incomplete, the court is hesitant to write the obligations for the parties, unless it has a mandate to do so, either under some limited statutory control, or by implication of terms under common law. Thus the court's ultimate role is to give effect to the parties' intention and those freely undertaken obligations are ring fenced by individualistic ethics. This is true with regard to the pre-contractual phase and the performance phase.

For the purpose of this work I will divide the discussion into two phases: (1) the pre-contractual phase, (2) the contract phase. There is obviously the post-contractual phase, which might touch on the issue of legal certainty, but not to a great extent.

2. The pre-contractual phase

In the first phase, the court is only willing to police positive bad faith behaviour of any of the parties. Some positive action is required in order to impugn the agreement, ie. a misrepresentation (statement of fact or conduct). Moreover, there is no general duty of disclosure under English contract law Keates v Cadogan (1851). There are exceptions however, for instance a duty of disclose may arise where the relationship between the parties rises up to a relationship of trust and confidence, as in the case of contracts of the utmost of good faith (uberrimae fide).

It is well established that English contract law does not recognise a general duty to negotiate in good faith. This was described by Lord Ackner in Watford v Miles as 'inherently repugnant to the adversarial position of the parties involved in negotiations'. A duty to negotiate in good faith is too uncertain to be enforced. Nor the breach of which will it amount to a quasi tortious liability. The doctrine of good faith, however, may play a limited role in the formulation of the rules of contract law. A judge for instance can only subject an argument that appears to run contrary to the reasonable expectations of honest men to rigorous re-examination. (See Brownsword and McKendrick). Alternatively parties may insist under the contract that both parties use their 'best endeavours', which was held to be enforceable and which will impose a limited obligation on the parties to act reasonably and do what is commercially practicable in the circumstances (Rackman v Peek foods) [1990].

Moreover, preliminary contracts are less likely to be enforced under English contract law. The main reason is because it runs contrary to the adversarial nature of English contract law. For example parties might include in an agreement for the sale of land that it will be subject to a contract. Matters, however, become more complex where one party may wish to get a commitment of some sort from the other party that it will not back out away from the preliminary negotiations or that it would 'terminate negotiations with any third party or consideration of any alternative with a view to concluding an agreement with the other party'. In Watford v Miles it was made clear that 'lock in agreements' are not enforceable under English Contract Law and 'lockout agreements' are not enforceable if these are not certain, i.e. where the parties leave out any time limit on such an undertaking by one of the parties.

3. Incomplete and vague agreements

Uncertain agreements can be salvaged by effective interpretation of the parties' intention. Where there is a meet of the mind on all essential matters, which is objectively assessed, English law will enforce those obligations. The court would, however, approach the matter carefully so that they would not write the obligations for the parties.

English Courts have adopted a similar approach to incomplete agreements. 'Where there is a fundamental matter left undecided and to be the subject of negotiation, there is no contract', unless if there is an express or implied provision for its solution. (Courtney and Fairbairn 1975) (British Bank of Foreign Trade v Novinex [1949]. The rationale behind this understanding is that no court could estimate the damages because no one can tell whether the negotiations would be successful or would fall through; or if successful what the result would be (Furmston). Nevertheless, English courts would still enforce an agreement, despite its incompleteness, where the parties have commenced performance. The court in these instances would imply from the conduct (performing a service delivery of goods-Executed obligations) that, for example where the price has not been agreed, a reasonable sum is to be paid. In Terntham v Archital Luxer [1993] Steyn LJ said that: the fact that the transaction was performed on both sides will often make it unrealistic to argue that there was no intention to enter into a contract. It will often make it difficult to submit that the contract is void for vagueness or uncertainty. Specifically the fact that the transaction was executed would make it easier to imply a term resolving any uncertainty or, alternatively it may make it possible to treat a matter not finally established in negotiation as inessential. For example, where the price is not fixed by the contract as in the case of Sudbrook Trading Estate Ltd v Egglton [1982], and the contract specifies a mode for ascertaining the value or an agreement to sell at a value to be ascertained by valuers, the court will enforce the contract insofar as the mode of ascertaining the price is subsidiary and non-essential. Section 8 of the Sale of goods Act makes a similar stipulation, however, without making a distinction between essential or non-essential mode of ascertainment.

It is important to note that the court will be hesitant to make a contract for the parties. So where the agreement is uncertain, and where there is no objective criteria, or an existing standard, to ascertain either the quantity or price, the court will refrain from using the test of reasonableness in order to make a contract for the parties. Baird v. Marks and Spencer plc [2001]. In the latter case the agreeement was too uncertain that it amounted to an absence of an intention to create legal relations.

With regard to vagueness in Hillas v Arcos (1932) the HL construed a term allowing the buyer to purchase "100000 standards of softwood goods of fair specification for delivery during 1931" at a 5% discounted price as referring to, having regard to all the factual matrix of the case meaning, 'the output of the season 1930 and the classifications of that output in respect of kinds, qualities and sizes, something which can be ascertained if the parties fail to agree on.

An alternative approach to vague clauses is to sever these from the rest of the contract, and to hold the rest of the contract valid (Nicolene v Simmonds [1953]). The general approach as seen from the discussion above that English Courts are more willing to give effect to salvagable vague terms than they are willing to give effect to incomplete agreements, where the incompleteness concerns an essential term. (Andrew Burrows)

4. The contractual terms phase

4.1. The parol evidence rule

The rule is that where the parties have reduced their contract to writing it is not permissible to adduce oral evidence to add to, vary or contradict the written contract L'estrange v Graucob [1934]. The law commission emphasised that the 'parol' evidence rule is workable where the parties have intended that their written contract represents the 'whole of the contract'; where their intention is different then oral evidence or terms are permitted. This can be achieved by including a contractual term which would guarantee the entirety of their agreement. English Courts would give effect to the signature of the parties when used as a formal devise to manifest consent of the terms of the contract. The parties can avoid the harshness of parol evidence rule by, where possible, invoking the pronciple of non east factum (was signed in circumstances which made it not her act), or where the contract was not entered under ordinary circumstances (misrepresentation etc… (See procedural unfairness below).

Courts can, however, avoid the harshness of the parol evidence rule by employing the doctrine of 'collateral contract': 'An Agreement which was made before or at the same time as, but separately from, another contract, which if unintegrated can be supplemented by evidence'. Such collateral contracts, the sole effect of which is to vary or add to the terms of the principal contract, are viewed with suspicion by the English courts. Parties cannot use this doctrine in order to escape from the full performance of the contract which was entered into by them and undermine the authority of written contracts (Ecay v Godfrey). One may add that any laxity on these points would compromise the contractual certainty that the parties have bargained for.

4.2. Implication of terms

In recent years a number of competing theories have emerged as to the manner by which terms are implied into a contract under common law.[1] Clearly there is a correlation between the implication of terms and contractual certainty. The more stringent/certain the test which allows courts to imply terms into the contract the more certain agreements become. English law is not clear on this issue. It is more useful for contractual certainty that English courts limit the implication of terms into the contract to cases where it

1 There are other ways of implying terms into a contract such as by statutory implication, and implication by custom, and course of dealing.

would be necessary to give business efficacy to the agreement and nothing short of it (see Moorcock (1889) for the necessity test). This would be a triumph for contractual certainty. Terms can, however, be implied by the courts into contracts of a particular type. Tenancy agreements… Employment contracts etc… in this instance it was argued, (unclear whether this is the correct approach) that terms should be implied if this would give effect to the reasonable expectation of the parties, and would be fair under the given circumstances (Crossly Faithful[2004 See also Equitable Life Assurance Society v Hyman (2000). For example, in Nash [2001] v. Paragon Finance Plc the Court of Appeal implied a term in secured loan agreements to the effect that the rates of interest would not be set dishonestly, for an improper purpose, capriciously or arbitrarily. Under the latter test consideration of contractual fairness overrides business efficacy or business logic.

Having said that English courts have consistently upheld that when implying a term under common law, the court in effect is expressing the real intention of the parties. Additionally, any implication must comply with two conditions:

- the term must be capable of close expression;
- must not contradict any express term of the contract (BP Refinery 1978).

4.3. Classification of terms

It was early recognised that contractual undertakings were of two different kinds: those collateral to the main purpose of the parties as expressed in the contract, and those which were mutually dependent so that the non-performance of an undertaking of this class was an event which excused the other party from the performance of his corresponding undertakings (Hong Kong fir Shipping per Lord Justice Diplock [1962]). The first kind is referred to as warranties and the other type is referred to as conditions. A clear classification of terms would increase the certainty of agreements. Contractual certainty mandates an approach where the classification of terms depends on the nature of the term, which would lead to remedial rigidity (traditional approach). This has been the traditional approach. However in Hong Kong Fir Shipping [1962] the English court departed from the traditional approach and employed an approach which focused on the consequence of the breach, leading to remedial flexibility. The more serious the consequence of the breach, the more likely that the term will be treated as a condition. This middle group is called 'innominate' or 'intermediate' terms. The House of Lords in the Hansa Nord [1976] confirmed this approach. One must note that this approach leads to contractual fairness whilst stabbing the idle (contractual certainty or individual ethics) in the back.

4.4. *Procedural v substantive fairness*

As explained earlier English contract law does not recognise a general duty of good faith (Watford v Miles).

As a consequence notions of critical justice, or requirement of fairness, or positive cooperation run contrary to the ethics of English Contract Law. English law is readily prepared to regulate procedural unfairness, less likely, however, to regulate substantive unfairness. Many common law doctrines have immerged which control vitiating circumstances, such as the doctrine of undue influence, economic duress, unilateral mistake, misrepresentation. Contractual certainty thus is reinforced and is likely to survive leave where one of the parties exert some illegitimate pressure or abuse a relationship of trust and confidence at the time of entering into the agreement. Moreover, English contract law, despite the famous dictum which was made by Lord Denning in Lloyds Bank Ltd v Bundy [1974], does not recognise a general doctrine of unconscionabilty or a doctrine of inequality of bargaining power. This dictum was robustly rejected by the Court in the famous decision of National Westminster Bank plc v Morgan [1985], and in other leading cases. Lord Scarman said that 'the parliament has undertaken the task (and it is essentially a legislative task) of enacting such restrictions on freedom of contract as are in its judgment necessary to relief against the mischief'. Thus substantive fairness is given effect by Statutory control, such as the Sale of Goods Act 1979, and the Unfair Contract Terms Act 1977. It is important to note at this point that this approach is more so robust in Business to business (B2B) contracts.

Other issues which may be relevant to contractual certainty:

- Supervening events: English courts are hesitant to discharge agreements;
- Common mistake: same as above, very cautious unless there is a mistake about a fundamental matter... (Bell v Lever).

5. Conclusion

English judges prefer to think in absolute logic (as opposed to relative logic), thus preferring a paradigm where contractual certainty is the rule rather than the exception. This, however, is not possible where business realities require a dynamic system which could regulate contractual failure, such as incompleteness, vagueness, frustrating events etc. To do so English law has developed a piecemeal approach responding to contextual challenges. At all time it has preserved the overriding principle of contractual freedom, and contractual certainty, and only compromising the latter where it is imperative to do so, or where the parliament has interfered by introducing statutory control. Thus where individualistic ethics are preserved so does the contractual certainty; whether this is the ideal, remains to be a personal passion of mine which I feel falls outside the scope of this research.

Marios Koutsias*

COMPARING COMPANY LAW

1. Introduction

This chapter will focus on legal certainty and company law. It will attempt to shed light on aspects of English company law which are marked with such a degree of lack of clarity that issues related to their interpretation are raised. The English legal system is one of the most prominent legal systems at international level. It has been shaped through many centuries and thrived on the basis of very distinctive principles such as the pivotal role played by the judiciary and the relatively limited in relation to continental European jurisdictions employment of legal codes and statutory instruments. The ability of the judicial authorities to shape rules and provide their own interpretation of the existing statutory texts has led to a system which is marked by an impressive level of flexibility with a judiciary that in practise complements the existing legislative framework with its rulings to a degree that cannot be detected in civil law jurisdictions.

Company law could evidently not constitute an exception to this rule. When one refers to company law one refers to a body of jurisprudence and statutes which have evolved continuously over centuries. English company law follows the general trend and has established itself as point of reference for international lawyers; it is a jurisdiction whose regulatory and in many ways cultural influence has crossed the national borders to transcend the laws of divergent nations across the globe as a testament to the country's impressive legal heritage. The UK has therefore emerged as one of the most attractive destinations for investment as it provided potential investors with the dual benefits of a solid company law which granted to them an attractive degree of flexibility; English company law is centred around two basic principles that stand at the heart of every investor: the sanctity of the right to property and the almost religious adherence to contractual obligations. Both principles have rendered the country a safe haven for international investment and a destination attractive enough to convince companies from around the world to establish themselves in Britain.

* University of Essex.

English company law, however, remains distinctive in the fact that the very principles on which it is based – the sanctity of property and contracts – present certain particularities within its context. The application of both concepts at company law level as it is argued in this chapter has been proven to be an issue which is if not problematic and controversial at least open to a variety of debates and conflicts.

As it is going to be clearly explained in this chapter the notion of the company as a contract forms the basis on which the institutional arrangements within the corporation are shaped. The place of shareholders and their relation with the directors are viewed under this angle. The contractual nature of the English company provides the regulatory basis for its internal institutional setting which will comprise as its main actors the shareholders and as a significant factor the directors. The relationship between the two is defined by the definition of the company as a contract. The problem as it is thoroughly explained is that this contract is of a very peculiar nature and therefore it subsequently impacts on the shaping of the balance between the two aforementioned groups. In addition to that the English company operates on the basis that shareholders are the actors of uppermost importance in the corporate context because they own the company; they have a property right to it. Again, as it is going to be demonstrated in this chapter, the notion of property is applied within the specific company law context in a rather problematic way undermining the prominence of the shareholders as the exclusive owners of the company; it sheds a few shadows on what should have been clear from the outset; the precise definition of what a company is and the shaping of a clearly discernible relationship between the shareholders and the company.

This is reflected at many aspects of company law; however the purpose of this chapter is to focus upon minority shareholder protection and more specifically on the application of Section 994 of the Companies Act 2006, which was designed in its statutory form to be an effective tool in the hands of an aggrieved shareholder against a director involved in some form of mismanagement. Despite the existence of a clearly drafted statutory provision in practise the courts have obscured its exact scope of application and in the end its very meaning with a set of decisions that have introduced additional requirements to the statutory provision and therefore somehow undermined the initial intentions of the legislators. The introduction and the interpretation granted by the courts of concepts such as those of "unfair prejudice" and "legitimate expectations" which form a key element for the application of the provision in question diluted the initial clarity of the relevant provision and raised questions as to its exact and precisely defined scope of application.

The thesis of this chapter is that the intervention of the courts in the implementation of section 994 of the Act has been so extensive and far-reaching that it has diluted the certainty as to its exact scope of application. The introduction of additional requirements centred around the aforementioned concepts has added a layer of uncertainty to both academics and practitioners as to the nature of the concepts involved as the judicial rules accompanying section 994 appear to lack the solidity necessary at the level of shareholder remedies. It is argued that the controversy which lays at the foundations of the English company law impacted on the nature of the interpretation that the courts have granted to section 994. The judges' intervention in a field of law founded upon principles such as property and contract which are distinctively controversial as to their application within the specific context has not contributed to allaying the risk of further legal uncertainty but it achieved quite the opposite; to blur the scope and basis of application of a statutory provision which was otherwise clear as to its wording and reach.

2. The nature of the company in the UK: the company as a contract with property rights in its centre

The theoretical conception on the basis of which the English company is based is the so-called 'nexus of contracts' theory.[1] Academics and legal researchers have looked at this theory either independently or in conjunction with the agency theory. According to this theory, the company is simply a nexus of contracts renegotiated by the individuals involved in it, with the principal aim of maximising their own utility[2] and the market value of the company through 'allocative, productive and dynamic efficiency'.[3] "Freedom of contract is an important issue in company law...one of the key questions is whether the law should impose mandatory rules on the private arrangements that govern companies and their shareholders".[4] The theory's main principle is the fact that companies as other organisations are 'simply legal fictions which serve as a nexus of contracting relationships among individuals';[5] they consist of many 'different kinds of relations that are worked out by those voluntarily associating in a company'[6] and they form 'the substance of the corporate fiduciary duty'.[7] More specifically, the private firm is 'characterised by the existence of divisible residual claims on the assets and cash flows of the organisation which can generally be sold without permission of the other contracting individuals';[8] hence shareholders have 'the greatest stake in the outcome of the company'[9] and therefore the greatest interest in 'the right of control above any other stakeholders'.[10] The natural outcome of this theoretical construction is the fact

1 Dine Janet, Koutsias Marios, *The Nature of Corporate Governance, The Significance of National Cultural Identity*, Edward Elgar, 2013, p. 98.

2 Alchian, A. and H. Demsetz, 'Production, Information Costs and Economic Organisation' (1972) 62 *American Economic Review* 777 and see Cheffins (1997).

3 Mayer, C., 'Corporate Governance, Competition and Performance' (1997) 24 *Journal of Law and Society*, pp. 152 and 155.

4 Ryan L. Christopher, Reece-Thomas Katherine, Section 459, public policy and freedom of contract: Part1, Company Lawyer, 2001, 22(6), page 177.

5 Jensen, M. and W. Meckling, 'Theory of the Firm: Managerial Behaviour, Agency Costs and Ownership Structure', (1976) 3 *Journal of Financial Economics* 305, p. 310.

6 Easterbrook and Fischel, 'The Corporate Contract' (1989) 89 *Columbia Law Review* 1416, p. 1426.

7 Smith, T., 'The Efficient Norm for Corporate Law: A Neotraditional Interpretation of Fiduciary Duty' (1999) 98 *Michigan Law Review* 214, p. 217.

8 Jensen, M. and W. Meckling, 'Theory of the Firm: Managerial Behaviour, Agency Costs and Ownership Structure', (1976) 3 *Journal of Financial Economics* 305, p. 311.

9 Macey, R.J., 'Fiduciary Duties as Residual Claims: Obligation to Nonshareholder Constituencies from a Theory of the Firm Perspective' (1999) 84 *Cornell Law Review*, p. 1267.

10 Van der Weide, M.E., 'Against Fiduciary Duties to Corporate Stakeholders' (1996) 21 *Delaware Journal of Corporate Law*, p. 57.

that since the company is a 'collection of private contractual relationships',[11] it is devoid of any social responsibility and should be left remote from any regulatory interference which would place limitations upon the right to use the free enterprise tool as shaped exclusively by its signatory parties. The economic analysis embarks on the perspective that the company has 'traditionally been thought of more as a voluntary association between shareholders than as a creation of the state'.[12] Neo-classical economists including Coase have viewed companies as method of 'reducing the costs of a complex market consisting of a series bargains among parties',[13] rendering unnecessary further regulation, especially on the part of the state. The focus is therefore clearly placed on contract as the 'mechanism which brings about exchange',[14] and the company is viewed as possessing a central position in 'the contractual arrangements of all other inputs'.[15] However, even if a purely contractual basis for the company is utterly accepted, it can be hardly viewed as independent from its regulatory background. The governance of corporations is effectuated not only through contracts, law and norms but also through the complex set of relationships that exist among these three sources of corporate governance. Contracts are written under the 'shadow of the state'… thus rules, norms and statutes inform the content of contracts that affect corporate law and corporate governance because they dictate the background factors that the parties take into account when they negotiate.[16] This theory focuses on deregulation by the state, but the construct of contract also has dubious roots especially aligned with the Kaldor-Hicks efficiency doctrine.[17] The lack of detailed statutory provisions grants to the courts a greatest scope of discretion as to not only the interpretation of the relevant statutory framework but also the ability to fill in the legislative gaps. And while this creates an environment which could potentially emerge as a particular friendly for business activities, it may have an effect on the clarity of the bundle of rules applicable in aspects of corporate activities. The wide ambit of interpretation left to the judicial authorities has led to the establishment of a new set of rules which however can be found if not conflicting at least notionally incompatible with the respective statutory provision such as the examined section 994. The introduction of new rules and criteria by the courts which are to be applied in the sort of situations falling within the ambit of section 994 places a certain layer of doubt over the precise rationale of the section in question. This issue is going to be analysed in detail at later parts of this chapter.

11 Fama, E., 'Agency Problems and the Theory of the Firm' (1980) 88 *Journal of Political Economy* 288, p. 290.

12 Cheffins B., *Company Law: Theory, Structure and Operation* (Clarendon, Oxford 1997), p. 41.

13 Belcher, A., 'The Boundaries of the Firm: the Theories of Coase, Knight and Weitzman' (1997) 17 *Legal Studies*, 22.

14 Alchian, A. and H. Demsetz, 'Production, Information Costs, and Economic Organisation' (1972) 62 *American Economic Review*, 777.

15 Ibid.

16 Macey, *Corporate Governance, Promises Kept, Promises Broken* (Princeton University Press, Princeton NJ 2008), p. 31.

17 Ogus, A., *Regulation: Legal Form and Economic Theory* (Clarendon Press, Oxford 1994).

Neglecting the regulatory, normative and societal background of the contractual arrangement will not therefore insulate the company from external influences and interventions. The latter are indeed inherent even in the contractual agreement which binds its members. Under this theory company law should have as its sole objective the maximisation of shareholder value; the shareholders are clearly at the centre of the company as the actors of maximum institutional value. To this end it must set default rules that maximise the efficiency of negotiating the nexus of contracts. In this way transaction costs can be reduced, as negotiations do not need to take place in every single transaction ... the emphasis is on investors' choices.[18] The corporation in this framework is to be understood as 'the product of a series of organisational innovations that have had the purpose and effect of economising on transaction costs'.[19]

The shareholders have a recognised 'residual claim' bearing the risk of somehow having the return of their investment being jeopardised while being the final actor to receive money from the company in the form of dividends, and after the remaining actors have been satisfied on the basis of their contract. The existence of this residual claim in conjunction with their character as the capital providers justifies their supremacy within the company context. The precedence of the claims of the other actors against the company betrays the contractual nature of their relationship with the company which guarantees returns for their labour, services or products supplied. The shareholders do not fit this model as comfortably as the other aforementioned actors; their relationship cannot be characterised as a contractual one from a purely legal point of view.

3. Is it really that clear?

In addition to that the widely accepted and vigorously supported view in the UK is that the shareholders are the exclusive owners of the corporation; despite the fact that this principle may appear to be unambiguous at first there are indeed a few aspects of the concept in question that would require further clarification. The decision-making capacity at corporate level is entrusted to the hands of the managers who take the decisions in relation to important aspects of corporate activity; however they cannot found any claim of ownership on the entity they effectively govern. The legal science is deeply precise, including an abundance of legal terminology with clearly defined concepts. Therefore, the owner of an object or property is in a position to control its possession and define its use. The owner of property can allow or prohibit the access to it, and can exercise the full rights of ownership on his possession. The sole right possessed by the owner of an asset is his ability to exclude others from the use of that asset. That is, the owner of a machine can decide who can and who cannot work on that machine, the owner of a building can decide who can and who cannot enter the building, the owner of

18 Lee, J., 'Shareholders' Derivative Claims under the Companies Act 2006: Market Mechanisms or Asymmetric paternalism?' (2007) 18 *International Company and Commercial Law Review* 11, p.379.

19 Williamson, 'The Modern Corporation: Origins, Evolution, Attributes' (1981) 19 *Journal of Economic Literature* 1537.

an insurance company's client list can decide who has and who does not have access to the list, and so forth.[20] 'The dictionary definition of ownership emphasises physical possession … it is a right which has no analogue in the case of an intangible asset or collection of assets.'[21] No property right is absolute, as Parkinson points out: 'Ownership rights are not absolute[22] (ownership of a knife does not entitle the owner to stab people with it). That shareholders might own companies does not mean that they may insist that directors attempt to maximise profits in any way at all.'[23]

In the company context, the shareholder does not own specific assets of the corporation but rather a proportional slice of the entirety of assets reflected in his stock certificate. 'Ownership of capital should not be confused with ownership of the firm.[24] 'Property, power and entitlement can be seen as the three central aspects of a share … a share is an item of intangible property. It is itself a "bundle of rights" giving the shareholder neither the ownership of the company's assets nor ownership of the company as a "thing".'[25] In contrast to the traditional legal theory of property rights, the shareholders are not in a position to exercise the traditional rights inherent in the concept of property; no shareholder is permitted to 'use a listed company's assets for his own purpose or restrict management's access to corporate resources'.[26] The concrete definition of the rights of proprietary nature stemming from the ownership of shares is indeed problematic, considering that the shareholders do not have a right to receive a fixed dividend nor to have their capital returned to them at a specified date. The difficulty in defining the exact scope of the proprietary rights stemming from stockholding is reflective of the challenges in defining shareholding in a traditional 'property right' sense. The corporate concept slices the bundle of rights inherent in property to various pieces; the stockholder 'gets the right to receive some of the fruits of the use of property, a fractional residual right in corporate property, and a very limited right of control. The rights to possess, use, and control the property go to the managers of the corporation'.[27] Thus, only the right to transfer the interest which has also been the overriding aim in the securities markets is 'unequivocally exercised by the stockholder'.[28] According to the court, 'a sole shareholder

20 Hart, O. and J. Moore, 'Property Rights and the Nature of the Firm' (1990) 98 *The Journal of Political Economy* 1119, No. 6, December, p. 1121.

21 John, K. and A. Silberston, 'Corporate Governance' (2005) *National Institute Economic Review*, August, p. 87.

22 For a detailed analysis refuting the justifications for unlimited property rights see J. Harris, *Property and Justice* (Clarendon, Oxford 1996).

23 Parkinson, J., 'The Socially Responsible Company' in M. Addo (ed), *Human Rights Standards and the Responsibility of Transnational Corporations* (Kluwer, The Hague 1999).

24 Fama, E., 'Agency Problems and the Theory of the Firm' (1980) 88 *Journal of Political Economy* 288.

25 Worthington, S., 'Shares and Shareholders: Property, Power and Entitlement: Part 1' (2001) 22 *Company Lawyer* 9, p. 258.

26 Caspar, R., 'Stakeholder Orientation versus shareholder value: a matter of contractual failures' (2004) *European Journal of Law and Economics*, p. 82.

27 Votaw in M.M. Blair, *Ownership and Control* (The Brooking Institute, Washington 1995), p. 224.

28 Monks, R.A.G. and N. Minow, *Corporate Governance*, 4th edn (John Wiley & Sons Ltd, Chichester 2010), p. 108.

has no independent right which is violated by trespass upon or conversion of the corporation's property';[29] an astonishing ruling that demonstrates the difficulty of using traditional notions of property in the corporate context.

While interviewed about shareholders exercising their rights, one institutional investor noted that "there is a weakness… in that responsibility for ownership rests with people who don't want it and are not seeking it. We are investing in shares because they give us a good return and it is coincidental really that they bring with them this responsibility. I am not saying we don't want this responsibility. I am saying it is difficult to handle that sort of thing".[30] That means that democracy as we know it at national level cannot be applied in the company context as the engagement of a vast number of shareholders, at least in large corporations, remains a complicated issue. Tocqueville's central hypothesis was that 'democracy constitutes the sole model of acceptable governance in modern society and it will eventually prevail in all spheres of organised activity';[31] corporations might prove even Tocqueville wrong, at least in the sense of democracy as we know it at the public domain. However, an additional conclusion is the rather unique nature of ownership in this context. If the owner cannot control what he or she owns, then it is not ownership in the traditional sense of the term as we know and experience it in the non-corporate world. Therefore, it can be validly claimed that the fervently supported exclusive ownership rights of the shareholders present certain particularities that render the whole issue more controversial or less clear than initially envisaged. The legal world might have to accept either that in the corporate context a new sense of ownership has to be constructed, or that shareholders do have a claim towards the company as they are undoubtedly and inexorably linked to it through their shares, but the particular nature of this relationship along with the far-reaching effects of corporate action at social level might require the consideration of other factors when designing the company policies and drafting its aims and targets. It is from the outset evident that if such controversy is detected at the very foundations of company law, further uncertainty can be traced at notions subsequently based on the relevant principles.

Despite that, their supremacy within the UK corporate governance model for example cannot be easily challenged. The Company Law Review Steering Group recognised the absolute dominance of shareholders in the company context requiring directors to 'manage the business on their behalf … the ultimate objective of the companies is to generate maximum wealth for shareholders'.[32] "Anglo-American corporate law embraces

29 *W. Clay Jackson Enterprises Inc v Greyhound Leasing and Financial Corporation*, 463 F. supp. 666, D.P.R. 1979, 670.

30 Solomon, J., *Corporate Governance and Accountability*, 2nd edn (John Wiley & Sons Ltd, Chichester 2009), p. 19.

31 Gomez, P-Y and H. Korine, 'Democracy and the Evolution of Corporate Governance' (2005) 13 *Corporate Governance* 6, p. 742.

32 Department of Trade and Industry, The Company Law Review Steering Group, *Modern Company Law for a Competitive Economy: the Strategic Framework* (1999), pp. 34–7.

a principle that has been expressed in one of the following ways: shareholder primacy, shareholder wealth maximisation or shareholder value".[33]

In the UK, the Companies Act 2006 in section 33[34] provides for the company's articles of association to bind the company and its members to the same extent, as if there were covenants on the part of the company and of each member to observe those provisions. In *Wood v Odessa Waterworks* (1889)[35] Stirling J said: 'The articles of association constitute a contract not merely between the shareholders and the company, but between each individual shareholder and every other.' Despite the fact that at first glance the provision appears to be clear enough to define the relationship between the shareholders on the one hand and the company on the other as contractual, the reality can be slightly less clear. The articles of association might be a contract that binds the company with the shareholders and provides the basis for the regulation of the relations among them as well, but this is no ordinary contract. According to the same Act in section 21, the company can amend the articles with a special resolution demanding a majority of 75 per cent of the members present and voting. This means that in contrast to other contracts, the one standing at the centre of the nexus is not one that requires the unanimity of its signatory parties to reform but can be done on the basis of a reinforced majority of the members who are present and voting. In *Allen*[36] yet another requirement was added by the court to the statutory provision when Lindley MR said: 'the power must be exercised, not only in the manner required by law, but also *bona fide* for the benefit of the company as a whole, and it must not be exceeded'. Therefore, quite uniquely in order to change the content of the contract, we do not need unanimity but a majority of 75 per cent along with the obligation to act bona fide for the benefit of the company; a requirement that the courts have interpreted in a rather strict manner in any case. Furthermore, as a matter of additional importance the issue who can enforce this contract becomes an exercise in obscurity. The obvious reply to this question would simply be the signatory parties, namely the company and the shareholders. However, both the reality and the legal interpretation of the 'contract' have rendered this reply simply incorrect. While any other contract including the respective of the employees and the suppliers would be automatically enforceable on the basis of its distinctive provisions to the company on one hand and the employees on the other, the shareholders would need the assistance of a corporate lawyer to inform them whether they are in fact in a position where they can enforce rights stemming from the 'contract' or not.

33 Keay Andrew, Company Directors Behaving poorly: disciplinary options for shareholders, *Journal of Business Law*, 2007, p. 656.

34 See Dine Janet, Koutsias Marios, Company Law, Palgrave Macmillan, London, 2013.

35 *Wood v Odessa Waterworks* (1889) 42 Ch D 636.

36 *Allen v Gold Reefs of West Africa Ltd* [1900] 1 Ch 656.

4. Is it a regular contract?

This is a key area of company law which presents a great challenge for both lawyers and practitioners. The flexibility in the interpretation of statutory and judicial rules inherent the contractual nature of the company can present a certain quite significant by-effect; a certain degree of legal uncertainty in relation to both the boundaries of the repercussions of the purely contractual basis of the company as well as the precise definition of the impact of the contract on the actors who are at least theoretically involved in it; mainly the shareholders. The definition of the English company as a contract does not entail a definition of the latter under standard contract law as it was analysed above. The company constitutes a contract but of a quite peculiar nature which poses a challenge on our ability to accurately define the balance of the internal institutional arrangements of the company. There is a certain degree of legal uncertainty for example which is linked with the question as to who can enforce the rights stemming from the articles of association which is the basic contractual agreement on the basis of which the company is based.

The courts have not been very helpful in providing us with a clear interpretation of the concepts in question. In *London Sack*[37] Scott LJ said that the contract, which was created between the members under the predecessor to section 33, did not constitute a contract between them 'about rights of action created entirely outside the company relationship such as trading transactions between members'. Great confusion was also created when despite what was initially thought, shareholder *could not* actually enforce the 'contract' when they were wearing an additional hat. So, even when they are also shareholders, directors of the company or its solicitors might find it difficult to enforce rights stemming from the 'contract'. In such case they are considered 'outsiders' and the courts refuse to grant them the rights provided for by the document that is otherwise taken to be a contract. In *Eley*,[38] the court held that the articles were a matter between the shareholders among themselves or the shareholders and the directors. They did not create any contract between a solicitor and the company. This was so even though the solicitor had become a member of the company some time after the articles had been signed.

This means that there is a subtlety in the definition of an 'outsider' in these circumstances. He is a person unable to enforce the articles or be affected by the contract in the articles. When the person seeking to enforce the articles has effectively two relationships with the company, he may be both an 'outsider' in the sense discussed in *Eley*, but at the same time a shareholder of the company. In this case he might find it difficult to enforce the articles. In *Hickman*,[39] Astbury J cited a number of cases and went on to say: "An outsider to whom rights purport to be given by the articles in his capacity as outsider, whether he is or subsequently becomes a member, cannot sue on those articles treating them as contracts between himself and the company to enforce those rights. Those rights are not

37 *London Sack and Bag v Dixon* [1943] 2 All ER 763.
38 *Eley v Positive Government Security Life Association* (1876) 1 Ex D 88.
39 *Hickman v Kent and Romney Marsh Sheepbreeders* [1915] 1 Ch 881.

part of the general regulations of the company applicable alike to all shareholders and can only exist by virtue of some contract between such person and the company, and the subsequent allotment of shares to an outsider in whose favour such an article is inserted does not enable him to sue the company on such article to enforce rights which are … not part of the general rights of the corporations as such. Therefore, shareholders of this kind would need an additional contract to enforce those rights.

To add further confusion, the court ruled in *Salmon*[40] that Salmon who was a managing director was able to enforce his right of veto by way of the contract in the articles. Here the court effectively supported that every shareholder has the right to enforce the articles of the company; a shareholder who also holds a position as an outsider (such as managing director, solicitor, etc.) can, wearing his shareholder hat, enforce the contract in the articles, even if the direct result of that enforcement is of benefit to him wearing his outsider hat. This analysis proves that the consideration of the relationship between the company and the shareholders as contractual could prove to be a challenging issue, accompanied by complicated questions that still need to be resolved. The nature of the contract binding the company with its shareholders presents certain particularities which render its inclusion in this nexus of contracts problematic for lawyers, to say the least. And if such a level of uncertainty and lack of clarity exists at the very foundations of English company law, it is evident that an equal level of uncertainty will accompany certain aspects of its function which emanate directly from the concepts in question.

The two lines of rulings demonstrate the difficulties encountered when attempting to treat the articles as a typical contract within the framework of contract law. In contrast, the document regulating the internal affairs of the company and the relationship among its components is distinctive, giving birth to rights and obligations that are consequently unique. Recognition of this principle is instrumental for an understanding of the position of directors within the British company and within the framework of the British company law.

It is therefore evident that the position of the shareholders in this contractual equation will also need further legal clarification. In *O'Neil*[41] the company was defined as 'an association of persons for an economic purpose … the terms of the association are contained in the articles of association'. Therefore, the company has an economic purpose 'agreed to by those persons constituting its composite members'.[42] By buying shares, one can therefore become a party to this agreement respecting the purpose of the association, agreeing to its terms and accepting its limitations but also taking advantage of the right to participate in the majority required to alter the terms of the agreement. This is integral in the notion of membership, but whether a contractual nature can be granted to those

40 *Quin & Axtens Ltd v Salmon* [1909] AC 442.

41 *O'Neil and another v Phillips* (1999) UKHL 24, [1999] 1 WLR 1092.

42 Bolodeoku, O.I., 'Economic Theories of the Corporation and Corporate Governance: a Critique' (2002) *Journal of Business Law*, p. 418.

rights and obligations is an issue that would require more solid legal justification. In this framework the employees, the suppliers or the creditors appear to have a clear contractual relationship with the company while the shareholders have a recognised residual claim in the sense that they have invested money in the company, assuming the risk of seeing no return of their investment. They are the last actor in the list to receive money from the company, usually in the form of dividends in case of profitability and after the employees have been paid on the basis of their employment contract. In fact, a shareholder appointed to directorship will not be entitled to receive a salary if this is not provided for by a separate employment contract; in *Re George Newman*[43] it was clarified that appointment to a directorship does not entitle one to be paid, even if he does in fact work for the company.

Fama claims that 'as residual claimants the shareholders guarantee the performance of their contracts by putting up wealth ex ante with this front money used to purchase capital and technology that the corporation uses for its productive activities'.[44] Therefore, the shareholders bear the residual risk but own the capital of the company and the technology therein, but not the company itself which retains its independence as a separate legal person. This statement 'is a first step towards the understanding that control over a firm's decisions is not necessarily the province of its shareholders',[45] as the 'ownership of the residual claim on the corporation's assets and earnings... is not the same as ownership of the corporation itself'.[46]

5. The directors within this framework: accountability in focus

The position of directors within the English company is therefore evidently defined by the nature of the agreement on which the operation of the company is based. The articles of association enjoy a central constitutional role in the internal affairs of the company. Section 17 of the Companies Act 2006 explicitly refers to the constitution of the company as the document which comprises the articles of association, along with any special resolution that have altered their provisions in the course of the company's life and operation. More importantly, as explained above, section 33 clarifies that the provisions of the articles bind the company and its members to the same extent as if there were covenants on the part of the company and of each member to observe those provisions. The terminology employed is also of particular importance; the Companies Act does not make a reference to the 'shareholders' at this point nor throughout its entire text. Instead, the preferred term is 'members'. This clearly betrays the predominant faith to shareholder primacy along with the legislative acceptance of the fact that they form the exclusive

43 *Re George Newman and Co.* [1895] 1 Ch 674.
44 Fama, E., 'Agency Problems and the Theory of the Firm' (1980) 88 *Journal of Political Economy* 288.
45 Fama, E., 'Agency Problems and the Theory of the Firm' (1980) 88 *Journal of Political Economy* 288.
46 Bainbridge, M.S., *The New Corporate Governance in Theory and Practice* (Oxford University Press, Oxford 2008), p. 32.

membership of the company on the basis of their property right. The Act leaves no doubt whatsoever in relation to that.

The company is indeed a contract which binds its members, and that means the shareholders despite the confusion arising when they also wear a directorial hat as it was thoroughly explained above. Therefore, the foundation of the internal management system on the basis of which the English company operates has a contractual basis. The articles form the contract that regulates the relationship between the company and the shareholders on the one hand and the relations between the shareholders among them on the other.

Adam Smith wrote in his monumental book, *The Wealth of the Nations:* Being the managers rather of other people's money than of their own, it cannot well be expected that they should watch over it with the same anxious vigilance with which the partners in a private copartnery frequently watch over their own. Like the stewards of a rich man, they are apt to consider attention to small matters as not for their master's honour and very easily give themselves a dispensation from it.[47] The agency theory[48] which is relevant in this context is set in the context of the separation of ownership and control which is a distinctive feature of the English (public) company. The analysis of Berle and Means[49] stands at the very core of this theory. The rapid evolution of the corporation from the joint stock company into the public company of the last century with a shareholding held by millions had led to what has been described as the separation of ownership from control; the shareholders are deemed as the owners of the company who however are facing the problem of controlling what they are deemed to own. A separate management is actually running the company and taking all crucial decisions with the shareholders 'best suited to discipline directors'[50] when conducting their duties but failing to effectively monitor their activities and challenge the legitimacy of their decisions. The theory focuses on the components of the relationship, namely the shareholders and the managers, and identifies an agency relationship; the shareholders are the principals who delegate duties to the other party to the relationship, the managers. The problems arising are mainly centred on the managers and their increasing autonomy brought by the waning of links between themselves and their principals. The agents are supposed to represent the principals and pursue their interests, but in practice the relationship has proven more problematic as the increasingly independent and insufficiently monitored agents availed themselves of the opportunity to promote their own agenda instead of serving the interests of the principals.

47 Smith, A., *An Inquiry into the Nature and Causes of the Wealth of the Nations* [1776] (Penguin, London 1999), Book V, Chapter 1, p. 26.

48 Jensen, M. and W. Meckling, 'Theory of the Firm: Managerial Behaviour, Agency Costs and Ownership Structure', (1976) 3 *Journal of Financial Economics* 305; Fama (1980); Fama and and Jensen, 'Separation of Ownership and Control' (1983) 26 *Journal of Law and Economics* 301.

49 Berle, *Power Without Property* (Harcourt, Brace & World Inc., New York 1959).

50 Matheson, J. and B. Olson, 'Corporate Law and the Longterm Shareholder Model of Corporate Governance' (1992) 76 *Minnesota Law Review* 1313, p. 1328.

This brings to the spotlight the necessity of introducing those 'institutional arrangements that would provide some checks and balances to make sure they do not abuse their power. The costs resulting from managers misusing their position as well as the costs of monitoring and disciplining them to try to prevent abuse have been called agency costs'.[51] The latter have to be added to the previously incurred 'residual loss' which is the reduction in shareholder value brought about by managerial behaviour that fails to fully incorporate shareholder interest in managerial decisions. The managers might be willing to assume extra risk to pursue their individual rights, sometimes leading to further residual losses for the shareholders. This is usually referred to as the problem of 'risk sharing'[52] which involves different agendas, diverse perceptions of risk and to a diverging set of interests. The agency theory offers shareholders 'a pre-eminent position in the firm legitimised not by the idea that they are the firm's owners but instead its residual risk takers'.[53] The shareholder primacy is founded upon the principle that it is the shareholders who assume the risks of their investment and therefore they should enjoy a status that would provide them with the appropriate guarantees. The shareholders who have entrusted the running of the company to managers might find themselves in a situation where not only are their interests not served in the best possible way, but due to managerial pursuance of self-interest they incur both residual and subsequently agency costs. Costs can include time-consuming efforts or meetings to acquire the information necessary for a more effective monitoring of the managerial group. 'It is generally impossible for the principle or the agent at zero cost to ensure that the agent will make optimal decisions from the principal's viewpoint.'[54]

Imposing a certain standard of behaviour in the form of directors' duties is probably the most prominent way of internal control on directors' powers. "While a number of authorities have distinguished the role of directors from that of trustees, it is clear that similar standards of fiduciary duties to the company apply".[55] British company law may accept the principle of shareholder primacy as one of its pillars and most distinctive features, but the apathy among shareholders is eroding their ability to exercise an effective control on the powers of management. Minority shareholders are therefore left with the choice to found their claims on either section 994 of the Companies Act 2006 – in case of private companies – when the company is being ran at an 'unfairly prejudicial manner' for their own interests, or to raise a so-called derivative action on the basis of sections 260–3. Until "the end of the second world war common law…provided little protection to a shareholder who had been treated unfairly but lawfully by the controlling

51 Blair M. M., *Ownership and Control* (The Brooking Institute, Washington 1995).
52 Shankman, N.A., 'Reframing the debate between agency and stakeholder theories of the firm' (1999) 19 *Journal of Business Ethics* 319.
53 Clarke, T., *Theories of Corporate Governance, The Philosophical Foundations of Corporate Governance* (Routledge, New York 2008), p. 5.
54 Jensen, M. and W. Meckling, 'Theory of the Firm: Managerial Behaviour, Agency Costs and Ownership Structure', (1976) 3 *Journal of Financial Economics* 305, p. 308.
55 Munoz Slaughter Carla, *Corporate Social Responsibility: a new perspective, Company Lawyer,* 1997, 18(10), p. 319.

group within the corporation". The guiding principle...was that of majority rule"[56] reflected at *Foss v Harbottle*. The two sets of articles have been applied and interpreted by the courts in a way that severely limits the ability of minority shareholders to exercise an effective control on the powers of the management. In the case of section 994, a remedy suitable for private limited companies, the basic aim of the shareholder who resorts to such form of protection is to avail himself of the opportunity that this set of articles offer, which is to release himself from the badly managed company while retrieving his investment. Its analysis is useful since it mirrors the dominant judicial attitude towards statutory provisions in relation to minority shareholder protection.

6. Section 994 under the spotlight

> **994 Petition by company member**
> (1) A member of a company may apply to the court by petition for an order under
> this Part on the ground –
> (a) that the company's affairs are being or have been conducted in a manner that is unfairly prejudicial to the interests of members generally or of some part of its members (including at least himself), or
> (b) that an actual or proposed act or omission of the company (including an act or omission on its behalf) is or would be so prejudicial.

The exercise of the remedy in question, which is by far the most popular form of minority shareholder protection in the UK, evidently results in the departure of the aggrieved shareholder from the ineffectively managed company rather than a change in the quality, style and methods of management that have led to the company suffering losses. Therefore, the successful invocation of the remedy of section 994 will result in the company getting rid of the protesting shareholder rather than the ineffective director who most likely would have breached the duty he owed to the company therefore providing the grounds for successfully resorting to section 994. The management can benefit from the aggrieved and protesting shareholder's removal from the company, which will effectively remove a potentially menacing thorn from the directors' side. Companies "come in all shapes and sizes, from the publicly listed multi-nationals to the "quasi-partnership".[57] Section 994 is mostly relevant with the context of the latter as it provides for the ability of a shareholder to be bought out of the company; in the case of publicly listed companies a shareholder is in any case in a position to sell his shares to third parties. As explained above the shareholder is viewed as the exclusive member of the company. Section 994 is centred around the notion of "membership interests".

56 McGuiness, Copp Stephen, Protecting Shareholder Expectations: a Comparison of UK and Canadian Approaches to conduct unfairly prejudicial to shareholders: Part 1, *International Company and Commercial Law Review*, 2000, 11(5), p. 184.

57 Grantham B. Ross, The doctrinal basis of the rights of company shareholders, *Cambridge Law Journal*, 1998, 57(3), p. 557.

"Membership is ultimately a contractual relationship".[58] The latter "incorporates the legal rights of a shareholder found within the company's legislation, at common law… and within the company's constitutional documents… in Foss v Harbottle the legal rights afforded to membership do not extend to provide a shareholder with a personal remedy… as this is vested in the company and the company alone. Nevertheless section 994 is concerned with membership interest…".[59]

If minority shareholders' remedies are all about assisting the shareholders to deal with cases of a breach of directors' duties which can lead to potentially significant losses, then the remedy in question has not only failed to deliver this aim, but has led to the directors removing an annoying source of complaints from their agenda. The minority shareholder might be able to release himself from the company on the basis of onerous requirements and reinvest elsewhere, but the company he left behind may sustain a failing system of management accompanied with an ineffective set of controls and checks. The practical inability to enforce a strict system of internal checks on the directors' actions even in cases of a breach of duty is a feature integral in the function and application of the British company law. The reading of section 994 independent of the courts' interpretation reveals a legislator who purported to grant this section a much wider scope of application; however "it has been left to the courts to define the scope of the protection afforded by these section"[60] and therefore its application by the courts as will be examined in this chapter has severely limited its ambit to an extent that could be found as conflicting with the initial intentions of the legislator. "The effectiveness of section 994 as a means of affording effective minority protection is in the main dependent upon the creativity of the judges when confronted with the concepts of unfairness and legitimate expectations".[61] And this may lead to a lack of clarity as to the exact set of rules and criteria to apply in a given case.

7. The unfair prejudice question

Sections 994–996 replace ss. 459–461 Companies Act 1985, providing a remedy for a member when 'the company's affairs are being or have been conducted in a manner which is unfairly prejudicial to the interests of its members generally or of some part of its members'. "The meaning of unfair prejudice has been variously described as opaque and elusive".[62] Consideration was given to the meaning of unfair prejudice in Re Bovey

58 McGuiness Kevin, Copp Stephen, Protecting shareholder expectations: a comparison of UK and Canadian approaches to conduct unfairly prejudicial to shareholders: Part 2, *International Company and Commercial Law Review*, 2000, p. 219.

59 Griffin Stephen, Shareholder remedies and the no reflective loss principle – problems surrounding the identification of a membership interest, *Journal of Business Law*, 2010, 6, p. 468.

60 Payne Jennifer, Sections 459–461 Companies Act 1985 in flux: the future of shareholder protection, *Cambridge Law Journal*, 2005, 64(3), p. 647.

61 Lowry John, The Pursuit of effective minority shareholder protection: Section 459 of the Companies Act 1985, 1996, *Company Lawyer*, 17(3), p. 67.

62 Griggs Lynden, Lowry P. John, Minority Shareholder Remedies: a comparative view, *Journal of Business Law*, 1994, September, p. 466.

Hotel Ventures (31 July 1981) unreported, quoted in *Re R. A. Noble & Son*[63] (Clothing) Ltd [1983] BCLC 273. Slade j said: 'a member of a company will be able to bring himself within the section if he can show that the value of his shareholding in the company has been seriously diminished or at least seriously jeopardised by reason of a course of conduct on the part of those persons who do have de facto control of the company, which was unfair to the member concerned.' He suggested that the test should be an objective one: 'would the reasonable bystander observing the consequences of their conduct... regard it as having unfairly prejudiced the petitioner's interest?' This text was adopted by the court in the R. A. Noble case. In that case a clear distinction was drawn between the prejudice which was held to have occurred and the unfair element which was not shown. In the case one of the directors had been deliberately and systematically excluded from the running of the affairs of the company. This was conduct which the judge found could have come within the section. However, the circumstances of each particular case had to be examined and in this case the director had brought his exclusion upon himself by disinterest. The conduct was therefore not unfair. This approach was adopted in *Re London School of Electronics Ltd.*[64] In *Re Macro*[65] the court held that where conduct was unfairly prejudicial to the financial interests of the company then it would also be unfairly prejudicial to the interests of its members. In assessing the fairness of the conduct the court had to perform a balancing act in weighing the various interests of different groups within the company. The court did not interfere in questions of commercial management but where the mismanagement was sufficiently significant and serious to cause loss to the company then it could constitute the basis for finding unfair prejudice. The concept of unfairness is thus capable of being a very broad one indeed.

In *Re A Company*[66] the court held that the acts of a shareholder in a personal capacity outside the conduct of the company's affairs were irrelevant. Thus the court was not interested in 'an attempt to blacken the respondent's name and to make the court look on her with disfavour as an immoral and attractive woman'. In *Re Red Label Fashions Ltd*[67], the respondent was alleged to be subject to disqualification proceedings as a 'de facto' director. Although she had been in business with her director husband, the court held that there was no evidence that she had assumed the role of director and exercised management responsibilities. She had acted 'as a dutiful wife' rather than as a director.

The concept of unfair prejudice is larger than the idea of infringement of legal rights. In *Re A Company*[68], Hoffman j said that in a small company 'the member's interests as a member may include a legitimate expectation that he will continue to be employed as a director and his dismissal from that office and exclusion from the management of the company may therefore be unfairly prejudicial to his interests as a member'. This is of

63 Re R.A. Noble & Son (Clothing) Ltd [1983] BCLC 273.
64 Re London School of Electronics Ltd [1986] Ch 211. Re Macro (Ipswich) Ltd [1994] 2 BCLC 354.
65 Re Macro (Ipswich) Ltd [1994] 2 BCLC 354.
66 Re A Company (No. 001761 of 1986) [1987] BCLC 141.
67 Re Red Label Fashions Ltd [1999] BCC 308.
68 Re A Company [1986] BCLC 376.

particular interest as the court appeared to have introduced an additional requirement to the statutory provision. Whilst section 994 is clearly to its reading and potential scope of application, the courts introduce a requirement which was not a part of the statutory text therefore blurring its precise reach as well as making its application more difficult and significantly more cumbersome. The establishment of the "legitimate expectations" requirement by the judicial authorities renders the interpretation of section 994 as a more challenging task as initially perceived.

The same view was taken in *Re Sam Weller & Sons Ltd*[69], where the court refused to strike out a petition alleging unfair prejudice by a failure to declare an adequate dividend. The court emphasised that 'interests' should be considered as wider than 'rights'. It should be noted that this wide view seems to be more easily adhered to in cases where a small company is involved, but it has recently been litigated in a number of sporting contexts. In *Re Tottenham Hotspur plc*[70], Terry Venables, the chief executive of Tottenham Hotspur, and Alan Sugar, its chairman, originally had a 50/50 interest in the company. Sugar later obtained control and Venables was removed as chief executive. Venables claimed that this removal was contrary to a legitimate expectation that Venables would be involved in managing the company. The court found that there was little if any evidence to support the allegation and did not make any order. In *Re Leeds United Holdings plc*[71] [1996] 2 BCLC 545 the court held that: 'The legitimate expectations which the court has to have regard to under s. 459 (previous numbering of the current section 994) must relate to the conduct of the company's affairs, the most obvious and common example being an expectation of being allowed to participate in the affairs of the company.' However, the court went on to dismiss the s. 459 action in that case because it was based on an expectation that a particular shareholder would not sell his shares without the consent of the other shareholders. This was held not to relate to the company's affairs and therefore fell outside s. 459.

Therefore, there has been "much judicial consideration concerning the issue of corporate wrongs litigated in the context of unfair prejudice claims, there remain considerable uncertainties as to the circumstances in which the court would grant a corporate remedy to the petitioning shareholder in an unfair prejudice claim... at least for now the uncertainty will remain. The difficulties encountered by the courts might seem to suggest that this is not an issue appropriate for incremental judicial development overtime but rather for legislative intervention in order to provide greater clarity and certainty to the law".[72] Section 994 "launches the courts on a discretionary voyage of discovery as the landmarks of established illegalities are obliterated on a judicial interpretation of what action amounts to unfair prejudice. As with all discretionary powers, there is always a question of the elasticity of its exercise, for occasionally judicial discretion may be

69 Re Sam Weller & Sons Ltd (Re A Company (No. 823 of 1987) [1990] BCLC 80.

70 Re Tottenham Hotspur plc [1994] 1 BCLC 655.

71 Re Leeds United Holdings plc [1996] 2 BCLC 545.

72 Cheung Rita, Corporate Wrongs litigated in the context of unfair prejudice claims: reforming the unfair prejudice remedy for the redress of corporate wrongs, *Company Lawyer*, 29(4), 2008, p. 103.

exercised arbitrarily in the absence of well defined parameters".[73] The problem here is that the concept of "unfair prejudice" is now a pre-requisite for the application of section 994 and the successful granting of the remedy in question to an aggrieved shareholder. However, the "foundation of an unfair prejudice claim as the breach of the agreement made between the shareholders and the company or the shareholders inter se … is construed in a very broad sense and includes any understanding held by shareholders … whether or not it is reflected in the formal constitution of the company".[74] And that "understanding" which may not have been included in the formal agreement is a fluid notion that can be interpreted and defined by the court almost on a case by case basis further blurring the already difficult to discern boundaries of section 994. The courts are left with a vast scope of interpretation that leads to a considerable degree of legal uncertainty as the rules to be applied are anything but fixed.

8. The legitimate expectations question

In "England the concept of "legitimate expectations" has evolved with relatively little judicial consideration being paid to its rationale during the course of its evolution".[75] The important case of *Re Saul D Harrison & Sons plc*[76]contains an extensive analysis of the operation of s. 459 (former section 994) to protect 'legitimate expectations'. Hoffman lj said:

'In deciding what is fair or unfair for the purposes of s. 459, it is important to have in mind that fairness is being used in the context of a commercial relationship. The articles of association are just what their name implies: the contractual terms which govern the relationships of the shareholders with the company and each other… Since keeping promises and honouring agreements is probably the most important element of commercial fairness, the starting point on any case under s. 459 will be to ask whether the conduct of which the shareholder complains was in accordance with the articles of association… Although one begins with the articles and the powers of the board, a finding that conduct was not in accordance with the articles does not necessarily mean that it was unfair, still less that the court will exercise its discretion to grant relief.

The term "unfairly prejudicial" was found as equivalent to the understanding of "oppression" in *Elder v. Elder and Watson*[77]: "A visible departure from the standards of fair dealing and a violation of the conditions of fair play on which every shareholder who entrusts his

73 Abugu E.O. Joseph, A comparative analysis of the extent of judicial discretion in minority shareholder protection litigation: the United Kingdom and United States, *International Company and Commercial Law Review*, 2007, 18(5), p. 188.

74 Paterson Paul, A criticism of the contractual approach to unfair prejudice, *Company Lawyer*, 2006, p. 133.

75 McGuiness Kevin, Copp Stephen, Protecting shareholder expectations: a comparison of UK and Canadian approaches to conduct unfairly prejudicial to shareholders: Part 2, *International Company and Commercial Law Review*, 2000, p. 219.

76 Re Saul D Harrison & Sons plc [1995] 1 BCLC 14.

77 Elder v. Elder and Watson (1952) SC 49.

money to a company is entitled to rely." The courts therefore are eager to look beyond and outside the actual contract – in the form of the articles of association – and to recognise an expectation such as the expectation to participate in the management. Whether "implicitly or explicitly the concept ... is given meaning by reference to the parties' ex ante understandings and expectations ... hypothetical bargains can be distinguished on the grounds of generality i.e. the extent to which they reflect the expectations and intentions of a collectivity of corporate actors...this means that section 994 gives effect to a hypothetical bargain characterised by a high level of generality".[78] It is only natural that at this stage generality is accompanied by uncertainty too as there is no pattern against which the legitimate expectations can be measured or assessed. "The difficulty now arises as to how to distinguish a petitioner's legitimate expectations which deserve legal protection from others which do not ... the scope of a court's power to grant reliefs under this section is extremely wide".[79] It "enables judicial interference in private bargains resulting in the imposition of judicial notion of fairness".[80] That judicial attitude however could be found as conflicting with the contractual nature of the company on the basis of which the English company is founded. If the latter is to be literally followed "individuals should be left to pursue their own preferences as much as possible ... the "invisible hand" of the market should be left to operate with as little governmental interference as possible as such interference would only serve to distort the market in which voluntary exchange takes place".[81] Therefore, it appears that this judicial approach may come into conflict with the principles which stand at the foundations of English company law even when the latter as explained above are not devoid of controversy and criticism.

The question in relation who has a legitimate expectation to participate in the management of the company is one which cannot be replied with any degree of certainty. Aside the shareholders who have been previously removed from management and they can therefore found a potential expectation to continue to be a part of it on the basis of their previous participation at the board, it is not clear at all which other parts of the shareholding can validly sustain such an expectation. There have been no clearly defined guidelines by the court as to who can claim such an expectation. And since the latter form a requirement for the section 994 remedy to be granted it is obvious that the application of the latter is based on obscure terms. Companies therefore are "affected ... by the uncertainty arising from a section 994 action ... the section has to be "all things to all people".[82] That is further supported by the view that in "listed companies the

78 Goddard Robert, Enforcing the Hypothetical Bargain: sections 459–461 of the Companies Act 1985, *Company Lawyer*, 1999, 20(3), p. 73.

79 Fang Ma, A challenge for China: is it possible to introduce unfair prejudice remedies? Part 1, *International Company and Commercial Law Review*, 2009, 20(12), pp. 419–420.

80 Atwal Harkamal, Self-interest, justice and reciprocity in unfair prejudice, *UCL Jurisprudence Review*, 2004, 11, p. 271.

81 Atwal Harkamal, Self-interest, justice and reciprocity in unfair prejudice, *UCL Jurisprudence Review*, 2004, 11, p. 274.

82 Roberts Pauline, Poole Jill, Shareholder Remedies – efficient litigation and the unfair prejudice remedy, *Journal of Business Law*, 1999, January, pp. 41–42.

court's approach will usually be that legitimate expectations of members are limited to compliance with the memorandum and the articles"[83] therefore they are strictly linked to the contractual agreement and its breach while not going above the contractual text.

Despite that section 994 is "at the forefront of the remedies available to protect minority shareholders from oppression".[84]

Hoffman lj goes on to point out that technically lawful actions may also be unfair:

'the personal relationship between a shareholder and those who control the company may entitle him to say that it would in certain circumstances be unfair for them to exercise a power conferred by the articles upon the board or the company in general meeting. I have in the past ventured to borrow from public law the term "legitimate expectations" to describe the correlative "right" in the shareholder to which such a relationship may give rise. It often arises out of a fundamental understanding between the shareholders which formed the basis of their association but was not put into contractual form, such as an assumption that each of the parties who has ventured his capital will also participate in the management of the company and receive the return on his investment in the form of salary rather than dividend.'

The judgment emphasised the fact that because the company is small, this is not sufficient to find that there are legitimate expectations above and beyond those in the articles. 'Something more' was needed and was absent in this case. It is clear that some evidence must be brought of an understanding between the parties separate from the articles. In *Re BSB Holdings*[85] the court made it clear that Re Saul D. Harrison did not mean that s. 459 was limited to cases of breaches of the articles or other agreements and that the categories of behaviour for which relief could be given were not closed. However, the court followed Re Saul D. Harrison in emphasising that 'fairness' meant fairness in a commercial context, which meant that directors had a duty to exercise their powers fairly between different classes of shareholders.

This case was affirmed in *O'Neill and Another v. Phillips*[86], which was the first case concerning s. 459 to come before the House of Lords. Therefore, "the terms "unfair" and "prejudice" have been termed as wide and general and the circumstances in which they can be applied cannot be delineated exhaustively".[87] "The glut of litigation caused

83 Sykes Paul J., The continuing paradox: a critique of minority shareholder and derivative claims under the Companies Act 2006, *Civil Justice Quarterly*, 2010, 29(2), p. 211.

84 Payne Jennifer, Sections 459–461 Companies Act 1985 in flux: the future of shareholder protection, *Cambridge Law Journal*, 64(3), p. 647.

85 Re BSB Holdings [1996] 1 BCLC 155.

86 O'Neill and Another v. Phillips [1999] 2 BCLC 1.

87 Clark Bryan, Unfairly prejudicial conduct: a pathway through the maze, *Company Lawyer*, 2001, 22(6), p. 171.

concern and *O'Neill* responded by adopting a narrow interpretation of unfair prejudice"[88] therefore, further narrowing down the ambit of section 994 by adding requirements to its application which go beyond the statutory text. Thus, the judicial "approach to unfair prejudice in the UK has undergone what has been described as a "conservative revisionism"... the manner in which unfairness was constructed (in *O'Neill*) ... might lead to cases of injustice".[89] In addition to that the existing case law on this matter demonstrates that "the court's approach to assessing the existence of unfairly prejudicial conduct is a result of their jurisdiction under section 994 which has an elastic quality which enables the courts to mould the concepts of unfair prejudice according to the circumstances of the case"[90] with an obvious impact on legal certainty. Lord Hoffman held that the existence of a quasi-partnership did not, of itself, give a right to a member to have his shares purchased; 'fairness' usually required some breach of the terms on which the member had agreed that the affairs of the company should be conducted. Section 459 had a very clear function and that was to protect shareholders against a breach of terms on which they had initially joined the company or from inequity in the sense noted by O'Neill.

9. Conclusion

Despite the existence of a clearly drafted section 994 in practise the courts have obscured its exact scope of application and in the end its very meaning with a set of decisions that have introduced additional requirements to it. The introduction or the interpretation granted by the courts of concepts such as those of "unfair prejudice" and "legitimate expectations" which form a key element for the application of the provision in question undermined the section's clarity and raised questions as to its exact application. The thesis of this chapter was that the intervention of the courts in the implementation of section 994 of the Act has been so extensive and far-reaching that it has diluted the certainty as to its application. They added a layer of uncertainty as to the nature of the concepts involved as the judicial rules accompanying section 994 appear to lack the solidity necessary at the level of shareholder remedies. It was supported that the controversy which lays at the foundations of the English company law impacted on the nature of the interpretation that the courts have granted to section 994. The judges' intervention in a field of law founded upon principles such as property and contract which are distinctively controversial as to their application within the specific context has created further legal uncertainty and blurred the scope and basis of application of section 994.

88 Chiu H. Iris, Contextualising shareholders' disputes – a way to reconceptualise minority shareholder remedies, *Journal of Business Law*, 2006, May, p. 315.

89 Cheung Rita, The statutory unfair prejudice remedy in Hong Kong: Part 3, *Company Lawyer*, 2008, 29(11), p. 346.

90 Tang Julia, Shareholder Remedies: demise of the derivative claim?, *UCL Journal of Law and Jurisprudence*, 2012, p. 207.

PART II

LEGAL CERTAINTY IN PROPERTY TRANSACTION: A COMPARATIVE APPROACH

Camille Bourdaire-Mignot*
Aurore Chaigneau**

HOW TO AND WHY MEASURE THE EFFICIENCY OF REAL ESTATE TRANSACTIONS IN FRANCE?

Headnote

The World Bank's successive reports on the efficiency of national law have caused much ink to flow. Despite the fact that their shortcomings have been repeatedly emphasized, the international organisation continues with its annual surveys, having only amended its method marginally. And yet, the most vigorous objections call into question its approach. Indeed, certain presuppositions in relation to the economic analysis of the law are applied with the utmost naivety, and even with a certain bias. The results are biased by a lack of knowledge and a failure to understand the legal systems that are the very focus of the study. A change of approach was thus required. At attempt has been made to understand how the rules of law are integrated in the economic transaction via interviews with professionals specialised in real estate transactions conducted by French and overseas purchasers. The result is unexpected; the rules are greatly denounced. They hide the conflicts associated with the allocation of competences among the different actors involved in the transaction.

1. In the World Bank's *Doing Business 2014* report, France ranks 149th (out of 189) in terms of the transfer of property. This poor position is the result of the criteria chosen for the evaluation: delays and costs (evaluated here) inherent in the procedure of transfer of real estate property.[1]

The method adopted by the World Bank has been widely criticized since the launch of this classification in 2004.[2] The relevance of the indicators is subject to caution, while

* Lecturer at the Université UPOND (Université Paris Ouest Nanterre La Défense).

** Professor at the Université de Picardie Jules Verne (Amiens).

1 The final report lists French law in 38th place: *Doing business 2014, Comprendre les réglementations pour les petites et moyennes entreprises,* Banque internationale pour la reconstruction et le développement, 11e éd. 2013.

2 The approach is criticized in a book by the French association "Association Henri Capitant des Amis de la Culture Française": Les droits de tradition civiliste en question, vol. I et II, Société de législation comparée, 2006. – Also: Des indicateurs pour mesurer le droit? Les limites méthodologiques des rapports Doing Business, sous la direction de B. du Marais: Doc. fr. 2006. – B. Fauvarque Causson et A.-J. Kerhuel, Is Law an Economic Contest? French Reactions to the Doing Business World Bank Reports and Economic Analysis of the Law: American Journal of Comparative Law, vol. 57, issue 4, Fall 2009.

shortcomings concerning the questionnaires and insufficient data are legion.[3] In terms of the transfer of property, for example, it can be noted that the duration of the procedure is calculated starting from the beginning of discussions in France, but only starting from the actual sale in the United Kingdom.

The very purpose of this annual report has been the subject of debate, since it consists of encouraging poorly ranked countries to proceed with the necessary legal reforms to stimulate their economic activity. However, as has been pointed out, the fact that countries with a Common Law tradition are positioned at the top of the ranking is one way of encouraging others to follow their example. While this method is brutal, doubt has been permanently cast on national practices, among which figures the transfer of property in France. *Moreover, the specific role of the French notary/solicitor is not taken into account, while this institution durably limits conflicts about titles of property.*[4]

Countering this line of reasoning raises difficulties. Even a comprehensive and more thorough questionnaire would be unable to better overcome the methodological obstacles resulting from the complexity of the links between standards and practices. We thus initiated a comparative study on the transfer of property in France and the UK by polling those in the field.[5] In doing so, the criteria used by the World Bank appear all the less legitimate given that they are not even relevant to the economic agents themselves. A criticism of the method (1) must, to a certain extent, get away from the context established by the report's authors to more fully reflect on the decisive factors of a real estate transaction and on the role of the law in this choice (2).

1. Ongoing criticism of the method's line of reasoning

2. The World Bank's economic analysis of the law rests on two pillars of the *Law and Economics*[6] movement: an analysis in terms of duration (**A**) and cost (**B**). These are the

3 For a methodological criticism: S. Bollée, Y-M. Laithier, C. péres (dir.) *L'efficacité économique en droit*, Economica, 2010; before: B. Dumarais (dir) D. Blanchet, A. Dorbec, *Des indicateurs pour mesurer le droit? Les limites méthodologiques des rapports Doing Business, Doc. fr.*, 2006. D. Cohen "Du choix des critères d'évaluation à une conception de la fonction du droit" in G. Canivet, M-A. Frison-Roche, M. Klein, *Mesurer l'efficacité économique du droit*, LGDJ, 2005. For the same criticism about contract law L. Usinier Le rapport Doing Business 2012, la concurrence des systèmes juridiques et l'attractivité du droit français des contrats, *Revue des contrats*, 2012, no. 4, p. 575.

4 M.-A. Frison-roche L'utilité du notariat face à des marchés menacés par la crise, *Droit et Patrimoine*, 2011, p. 204; the author underlines the fact that the evaluation concerns the procedures more than the substantial law itself; also: M-A. Frison Roche, Acte authentique, acte de marché, *JCP N 2010, 1290;* L. Galliez Le notariat à la lumière de l'analyse économique du droit *JCP N*, 2010, no. 39, pp. 34–38.

5 This work, published in JCP N 2010, no. 37–38, 1273, was conducted on the occasion of the research contract on *"La modélisation comparée de la sécurité juridique" (compared modelling of legal security) (CEJEC and CRDP, M.-F. Nicolas-Maguin and B. du Marais, dir., université Paris-Ouest Nanterre La Défense)* funded by the *Mission de recherche Droit et Justice* public interest group as part of the programme dubbed "Attractivité économique du droit" (economic attractiveness of law).

6 For an overview of this movement (in French): R. Lanneau, *Les fondements épistémologiques du mouvement law and economics: thèse 2009,* sous la direction de M. Denquin, université Paris-Ouest Nanterre La Défense; Analyse économique et analyse juridique du droit: *Rev. recherche juridique* 2009–2, pp. 557–574.

two criteria for evaluating the efficiency of the transfer of property. The adjustment of the evaluation criteria since 2004 has in no way changed these two criteria.

1.1. *First criterion: transaction times*

3. The time taken to transfer property in France appears to be relatively long since it stood at 98 days in the Doing Business report published in 2010 and at 49 days in the report of 2014 (without any reforms!); compared with 40 for Germany, 12 for the United States and 21 for the United Kingdom in the Doing Business report of 2014.

France's 98-day period was obtained by adding up the durations of the following procedures: obtaining a building fact sheet from the mortgage registry, obtaining an extract of the land registry plan and other urban planning documents, establishing environmental certificates and diagnostics, the redemption of pre-emptive rights, the drafting of the deed by the notary and its publication in the mortgage registry. The said period is calculated starting from the signature date of the "promise to sell", whose option will subsequently be exercised.

For the United Kingdom, the 2010 report merely mentioned the transaction's registration in the land registry and the payment of taxes relating to the obtaining of the deed. So why is there such a difference when the actual transaction time is much longer?

By looking at the data for other countries such as Germany, we can see that the procedures examined are those involved in the actual property transfer. In Germany, the 40-day period includes the obtaining of an extract from the land registry concerning the property, the payment of taxes and the verification by the competent authority before the registration of the corresponding deed.

This data shows that the questionnaire is drafted in such a way as to obtain information on the time taken to obtain the deed rather than on the duration of the actual property transfer, in other words, on the duration of the economic transaction. Consequently, the French system, which separates the transfer of ownership from the delivery of the asset, or from the obtaining of the deed, is necessarily discriminated against. And yet, in Germany and the UK, real estate transactions also involve negotiations and prior deeds. Moreover, diagnostics and audits are also necessary in these countries. However, these facts and the corresponding time involved are omitted here because they take place before the transfer, whereas in France they are considered as taking place during the transfer, in the intermediate period of the "promise to sell". In fact, while the audits are generally prepared in advance – during the negotiations, they are often the object of precedent conditions allowing the purchaser not to bind himself in case of any defect. Of the three countries referred to, only the form on France mentions these conditions. If consideration were limited to the time needed by the notary to draft the deed of ownership and to register it with the mortgage registry, France would effectively make a great leap forward without having to engage in any legislative reform.

1.2. Second criterion: the transaction cost

4. The procedure in France *seems* too costly. In 2010, the cost of transferring real property was evaluated at 6.1% of its sales price, compared with 5.2% in Germany, and 4.1% in the United Kingdom. Among the top of the class are the United States, where the transaction cost *was* evaluated at 0.5%. Russia does even better (0.1%). Russian investors faced with a plethora of procedures, the financial outcome of which remains uncertain, will hardly be pleased.[7]

This rate is calculated based on the respective costs of the various compulsory procedures identified in each country. Logically speaking, the various taxes are integrated, along with administrative expenses and costs incurred by officers of the Court responsible for the procedure. However, no information is given as to the overall cost of the operation. While the questionnaire was completed by lawyers in all the countries concerned, the fees charged in their capacity as agents or consultants in the procedure are never specified. By focusing on the transaction's "administrative" cost, the authors of *Doing Business* have omitted to consider its "commercial" cost which, in a study of how business is done, is ironic to say the least. And yet, these costs are by no means negligible, especially for transactions concerning premises for professional use where it is common practice to call on the services of agents to search for a property, and on lawyers to perform an audit of this property and to prepare a possible offer or counter-offer of purchase. In this respect, dissociating the various costs is all the more delicate considering that it is often the lawyers who draft the pre-contract and who complete the necessary steps. In the UK, the lawyers effectively perform many of these steps and draft the deed. To conduct the comparison with all due reason, delimiting the object under study thus infers considering all the costs correlated to the transaction.

Such a reassessment would once again have a significant impact on the World Bank's table at a number of levels. It would effectively increase the costs accounted for in the most liberal systems in relation to those in systems where the intervention of public authorities is imposed. On the one hand, the fees of the other stakeholders can turn out to be fairly high, especially when they act alone and are, in fact, professionals essential to the entrepreneur. Under these circumstances, lawyers are better able to advise their client by verifying the origin of the property and the validity of the deeds, and to oversee the actual practice involved in the transfer of ownership. Their competence is a value which comes at a price.

On the other hand, the monopolistic system of the French notary, which is based on the principle of a lump sum payment (0.825% of the price), produces indirect effects. When formally presented, the system would appear to be extremely rigid since all transactions are subject to the same fee structure. In practice, however, this legislation allows a degree of compensation to be introduced between the various operations and, to a limited extent, a reduction of the transaction cost of certain complex operations such as those representing the sale of commercial property. In the first system, the lawyer is remunerated by the hour; in the second system, by the deed. Thus, in the

7 These data haven't been published in the 2014 report.

French system, the monopolistic position enjoyed by officers of the court guarantees their payment with standard and financial transactions, as well as the additional work needed to prepare and draft more sophisticated drafts. Furthermore, concerning very substantial transactions (over and above 80,000 euro) for which the fees are freely fixed, the notary will usually offer his or her client a discount to maintain that client's favour.

5. Practice in the French system thus varies significantly from the way in which it is often presented. In the opinion of those professionals who oversee transactions in different countries, the cost of the intermediaries who prepare the acquisition is not necessarily higher in France. However, systematic recourse to the notary always comes as a surprise to those unfamiliar with this institution in their own legal system, and prejudice concerning its cost is constant.

The reform of the transfer of real estate property in Russia since the change of political system offers an eloquent illustration.[8] In the mid-1990s, just as the notarial profession was being reorganised, it was decided that the notary would no longer benefit from his or her monopoly on the transfer of property, and that preference would be given to the principle of the transfer by private deed. The reason given was perfectly clear in this country renowned for its civil law jurisdiction: to avoid adding to the cost of the transaction in a difficult economic context so as not to hinder an emerging real estate market. Consequently, once the deed is concluded, it is registered by the purchaser or his/her court office representative according to a procedure that guarantees the legality of the transfer, and even the validity of the deed (a procedure similar to the one used in Germany). Nearly fifteen years later, the results are mixed and clearly reveal the pitfalls of short-term economic reasoning based on cost, a reasoning that was blindly adopted by the reformers of that period. In fact, no heed was paid to the country's specific context. And yet, in the 1990s, Russia was marked by a lack of any reliable banking system and by savings schemes that were made mainly in cash. Buyers and sellers who sought to go ahead with a sale had to carry the sums of money involved in suitcases, despite the fear of an incident. To try to ensure the proper performance of the transaction, the transacting parties had to rely on the services of well-established lawyers whose skills were not merely legal! It follows that the cost of these transactions increased accordingly. Russia's economic climate has since changed considerably, however. The possibility of giving back notaries the monopoly of the property transfer has been proposed, and a parliamentary bill is currently being debated. Those in favour are convinced that such a measure would mean substantial savings. It goes to show that the conclusions drawn from an economic analysis of legal rules are often reversible.

8 For an analysis of the reforms affecting property law in Russia, we will refer to previous works (in French): A. Chaigneau, *Le droit de propriété en mutation, essai à la lumière de l'expérience russe:* Dalloz, 2008.

2. How can the impact of the law on economic practice be evaluated?

6. The answer to this question is by no means straightforward. Similarly, merely stating the exact opposite of the World Bank's report to demonstrate that one notarial system is better than another is hardly satisfactory. A different slant can be attempted by questioning the appropriateness of the economic evaluation.

2.1. The appropriateness of the comparative evaluation

7. The justification offered by the report's authors is to encourage countries to undertake legal reforms. It thus boils down to improving legal performance based on duly designated indicators. The hypothesis used by *Doing Business* in terms of property transfer is based on a property sale between two limited liability companies with no foreign capital, for an asset comprising land and a commercial warehouse with an area of 1000 m2 owned by the vendor for 10 years.

Based on a purely local scenario, the authors thus hope to obtain information that can outline a relevant, international comparison. In fact, it is quite possible that certain procedures may appear to be outdated or excessively long in the light of progress made elsewhere. However, it is equally possible that certain procedures may incorporate practices and fees which more than make up for any weaknesses highlighted in a ranking table. The tendency to use comparatism as a justification and a means for reform is over-simplistic and, as such, potentially unfortunate. Indeed, the cumbersome nature of this comparative device can hide a systemic understanding of the law concerned and even produce effects that are the opposite of those expected.[9]

8. Finally, there is good cause to question the relevance of this international comparison with regard to real estate, a field in which legal practices are particularly localised. In fact, except when relocating overseas, the purchaser of a real estate asset does not consider the choice of applicable legislation. In practice, it is difficult for a purchaser to measure the inconveniences of a procedure, often caused by reasons subsidiary to the actual legal procedure itself. Moreover, criticism would require giving consideration to the detriments which purchasers are spared, such as uncertainty regarding the titles of ownership. This assumption is residual in French law, where the notarial practice has effectively done away with litigation.[10] Entrepreneurs in France do not appear to lament the existing procedure. In reality, the ongoing criticism of the procedure is driven by a concern to rationalise transaction costs, however the actors cannot guarantee that this cost would otherwise be any less. On the contrary, those working in international situations do not seem to consider the cost of the French procedure as a hindrance.

Consequently, the qualitative evaluation of these actors does not support the report's statistical conclusions. The difficulty to be had in formulating genuine criticism of a legal

9 B. Arrunada, Pitfalls to Avoid when Measuring Institutions: Is doing business Damaging Business? *Journal of comparative Economics*, 2007, 35 (4), pp. 729–747.

10 Cf. J. Tarrade, L'action des professionnels: le notaire, *LPA* 28 octobre 2004, 216 p. 17.

system can be explained by the gap between the scale of the assessment of the law and the scale of its practice.

2.2. *Changes of scale*

9. The economic analysis which used to focus on the study and theorisation of economic agents' behaviour has gradually shifted its focus to the rules of law. As confirmed by the protocol in *Doing Business*, from now on, the economist is interested in the rules themselves without having to consider their multiple interpretations and implementation, or, ultimately, the context in which they are used.[11]

The surveys show that this smokescreen is the result of foreign professionals who deal with law-related issues from their own legal viewpoint. The increase in international economic exchange has accentuated this phenomenon. The success of the economic analysis of the law naturally accompanies this increase. In fact, questions as to the appropriateness of national law can be raised for agents who genuinely have the choice to act on such or such a market. As important as their activities may be, they are still hindered by national rules. When the purchasers – and their advisers – of overseas real property are queried, it turns out that their view of the French legal procedure is much less problematic. This view is also reflected about the national lawyers with whom they work.

A number of foreign investors have set up their activities in France over the past twenty years or so. They have brought with them major consulting firms capable not only of overseeing acquisition procedures, but also of finding assets beforehand, negotiating their prices and conducting audits with other experts. The presence of the notary in France may sometimes seem incongruous for these investors, who are used to working with consulting firms that follow up their activities on all real estate markets.

The arrival of these firms has led to considerable change in the practices of real estate professionals. A due diligence procedure has been introduced to allow the interested parties to gather information on the property assets, to prepare a business plan and to obtain the necessary financing. This procedure was promptly adopted as a means of "rationalising" commercial practices and better regulating sales. The practice of the audit has since become widespread, consolidated by changes in national legislation. As a result of this preliminary phase, lawyers are expected to prepare all the necessary documents relating to the property's physical, economic and legal aspects. This in turn means that they are sometimes under the impression that they are doing the work of the

11 The knock-on effect of this approach is that it influences the lawyers themselves in the views in which economic justifications are found. For a study on these phenomena (in French): T. Sachs, *La raison économique en droit du travail, thèse LGDJ* mars 2013, tome 58. And for an analysis of the legal argument's constraints (in French): H. Muir Watt, *Les forces de résistance à l'analyse économique du droit dans le droit civil in L'analyse économique du droit dans les pays de droit civil*, dir. B. Deffains: *Cujas*, 2002, p. 43. – Th. Kirat et E. Serverin, *Dialogue entre droit et économie à propos des relations entre les règles juridiques et l'action in Le droit dans l'action économique*, dir. Th. Kirat et E. Serverin: éd. CNRS, 2000, p. 6.

notary. As a result, the notary's monopolistic position is a source of irritation, as it leaves the feeling of paying for work that has already been done.

However, the competencies of notary firms themselves have evolved to keep up with the changing real estate market. Some have developed services similar to those of other legal professions, whereby they participate in or accompany negotiations on the property. Their clients seem to have become used to the procedure, and effectively appreciate the absence of any litigation concerning deeds in France. Indeed, it was because of the possibility of this litigation that the due diligence procedure was adopted.

10. To conclude, a few paradoxes deserve to be raised. The economic analysis of the law has been driven by international players operating in a unique situation that cannot be compared to that of local players. Their practices have brought about certain changes to national practices, without necessarily challenging the prevailing legislation.[12] The attractiveness of the French real estate market is determined by fiscal, economic and financial criteria, since purchasers seek a financially profitable investment. The legal rules governing the purchase of a commercial real estate asset do not appear to present any difficulties, provided the titles of ownership are guaranteed. The *Doing Business* report thus misses its target; it calls into question a system on the basis of a deemed cost which, rather than being decisive, is marginal in relation to the overall economic reality. This is confirmed by all purchasers. However, it evades important issues such as the appropriateness of applying compensation for a notary's clients due to the marginal additional cost incurred by certain commercial transactions.

12 About the role of the practice, cf. The conference proceedings "Le rôle créateur de la pratique (dans la formation des juristes et dans l'élaboration de la norme", GP 18 avril 2013, no. 107–108.

Marie-France
Nicolas-Maguin*

OVERVIEW OF HOW A REAL ESTATE TRANSACTION IS CONDUCTED IN FRANCE

Assessing the legal security of a real estate transaction involves presenting the operation's various phases.

From the outset, we can stress the importance of the real estate transaction in our cultural and, consequently, our legal tradition. Associated with the law of contract in its technique, the specificity of the real estate transaction ties in with the nature of the property, which represents a portion of the national territory and, as such, one that is subject to the rules that fall under the authority of the State and its territorial communities. In this respect, we must emphasize the growing number of controls and restrictions that have been imposed upon the real estate market by the State since the second half of the 20th century, at a pace that shows no signs of slowing down. Any modification of real property infers an administrative authorisation. The prerogatives of the State and the numerous standards it imposes, for various objectives (land-use planning, environmental protection, etc.), beset any real estate transaction, and represent essential elements that have a profound effect on the value of the private property and the conditions of its transfer.

The prerequisite to the real estate investment is **the initial decision** which, in the context concerned, i.e. the purchase of an office building by a company, assumes that various factors are analysed (market conditions, economic growth, taxation, political stability) and that they have proven positive in the eyes of the investor. This decision is the starting point of the operation that involves finding a property asset corresponding to the selected criteria.

1. Searching for the asset to acquire/selling an asset

The search for a property asset can be carried out by an intermediary, the real estate agent, who will be **mandated to search for the asset** on behalf of the investor and/or the

* Maître de conférences des Universités.
CEJEC. Université Paris Ouest – La Défense.

vendor. The scope of the agent's mission may vary. As a minimum, it will entail searching for the asset. At the other end of the scale, it may include the negotiation and even the drafting of a pre-contract.

The vendor may also task the real estate agent with the sale of an office building by adjusting the scope of the mandate of sale.

The real estate agent's liability may be incurred if he fails to comply with his commitments, however, at this stage, the contract of sale has not been concluded.

2. Negotiation

The negotiation only starts when the investor is interested in a property for sale.

The participants in the negotiation are necessarily the investor/buyer and the owner/vendor. They may be assisted by a real estate agent or a notary.

The prospective purchaser makes an initial offer. If it is accepted, the purchaser benefits from a 3-week exclusivity period to have an audit report established, for which he or she receives all the documents relating to the building. This report is established by different professionals: technicians to assess the state of the building (ground conditions, building solidity and maintenance), lawyers (lease conditions and term of the lease, taxation, etc.) and a notary (title of ownership, surfaces, easements, purpose of the building, building permits, environmental constraints, leases). This report is forwarded to a real estate expert mandated by the investor for an assessment of the building. The amount of the offer to purchase will be based on this assessment.

There are different types of report; the most comprehensive state the property's positive and negative aspects, while those such as the "executive summary" merely state the weaknesses.

In addition to the negotiation of the price, the exclusivity period allows the purchaser to seek financing for the operation. The banks called on will in turn conduct their own audits, usually through a notary.

3. Drafting of the pre-contract (provisional sales agreement)

In France, the pre-contract is a key step in the real estate sale process.

This concept has a number of variants whose legal consequences vary considerably.

The most common is the **unilateral promise to sell** by which the vendor undertakes to sell the real property at a price stipulated in the deed for a set period. In return for this promise, the prospective purchaser pays a sum of money: the reservation fee/security deposit. During this period, the beneficiary of the promise can either buy the property, or he/she can relinquish it and lose the amount paid upon the signing of the pre-contract.

The synallagmatic promise, unlike the unilateral promise to sell, infers the dual consent to the sale: that of the purchaser and the vendor. The contract is formed; however its existence may be conditioned by the parties on the fulfilment of conditions precedent, such as the obtaining of an official authorisation or the obtaining of the bank loan.

In both cases, the completion of the sale depends on the fulfilment of the conditions precedent, which must not be dependent on the intent of the contracting parties.

Whatever its nature, the pre-contract can be drafted either by the parties' legal consultants (real estate professional, lawyer) or by a notary.

- **The pre-contract is drafted by the real estate agent** who brought the parties together, or by the parties' legal consultants.
  Here, the real estate agent proposes a standard "promise to sell" contract specifying the main characteristics of the contract of sale (the building's technical diagnostics must be annexed, art. L 271–6 CCH). The expert who established the diagnostics is required to take out insurance.
  Concerning office buildings, gas, lead and electricity diagnostics are not compulsory, whereas termite, asbestos, natural hazards and energy performance diagnostics are.
  The payment of a reservation fee or a security deposit is generally provided for. This sum of money represents between 5 and 10% of the price of the building. The real estate agent is authorised to receive this fee and to act as the receiver of the funds deposited.
  This pre-contract binds the parties and represents the first step in the completion of the sale. It must necessarily be transmitted to a notary, whose intervention is compulsory in respect of any real estate sale.

- **The pre-contract is drawn up by a notary.**
  At this stage, the notary must precede with certain legal verifications which will be included in the final deed and which guarantee the legal security of the transaction.
  He or she is thus required to check the **identity of the parties.** This goes beyond merely referring to identification documents; it implies obtaining – from the registration authorities (the town hall) – the birth certificates which additionally contain information on the family circumstances of the parties or on their legal capacity. The company's registration and the credentials of the body corporate's representatives must also be checked.
  Different **conditions precedent** will be provided for; their purpose varies depending on the legal status of the property and of the parties.
  - The authorisations required for the validity of the legal operation: authorisation of the guardianship judge for the legally incapacitated, permission of the spouse, specific authorisations for companies.

- New diagnostics, now mandatory, between the pre-contract and the final sale.
- The redemption of pre-emptive rights. If the town hall benefits from a pre-emptive right, a declaration of intention to dispose must be sent to it. The town hall has two months to reply.
- The condition relating to the loan, which is often excluded in transactions that concern office buildings.
- The condition relating to the follow-up of the audit if it continues during this phase.

Verification of the origin of ownership. The notary will check the chain of the real property's owners over a period of 30 years. For this purpose, he or she consults the mortgage registry, but must nevertheless check the concordance of the titles of ownership and their publication.

Verification of the mortgage statement. This operation serves to find out the security interests (mortgages and privileges) listed on the asset as securities for the vendor's liabilities. It may have to comply with the procedure used to satisfy creditors.

Condominium building. The regulations for co-ownership and the decisions resulting from the co-owners' annual general meetings must be included in the pre-contract.

The cost of the transaction includes different elements: besides the price of the building, it must state the negotiation fees, the various taxes collected for a real estate sale (capital transfer tax, possible capital gain).

The operation's financing method is stated. It is reminded that the loan may be subject to a condition precedent.

4. Signing of the authentic deed

Representing the last step in the real estate transaction, the authentic deed accounts for the transfer of the building's ownership.

It is necessarily drawn up by a notary and signed by the parties. The choice of notary is made by common agreement between the parties. Nevertheless, the vendor and purchaser may bring into play their own notaries, without increasing the cost since the two notaries must share the amount of the fees paid.

The notary who drafts the authentic deed is under an obligation to give advice in relation to the two contracting parties. His or her intervention guarantees the purchaser against the risk of eviction.

In addition to compulsory civil liability insurance, a collective guarantee by the notarial profession will consolidate the guarantee given to the client by the notary as a result of his or her intervention.

5. The transfer of ownership

The transfer of ownership takes place on the date of the signature of the authentic deed, which is given probative and binding force. The notary draws up a declaration of ownership and forwards the documents to the mortgage registry, which publishes the name of the new owner. The transaction then becomes applicable to third parties.

The notary is required to retain the original copy of the authentic deed, which he or she established, for 100 years.

Beyond this time, the deed is sent to the Departmental Public Archives.

In conclusion, French law guarantees the legal security of real estate sales through a number of rules which are compulsories. In addition, concerning the sale of real estate, the principle of the immediate transfer of ownership by the sole exchange of consent provided for by the Civil Code (art. 1583) is set aside. Worthy of note is the essential role of the notary, who intervenes to guarantee the legal security of the real estate transaction.

Peter Luther*

PROPERTY TRANSACTIONS IN ENGLISH LAW: GENERAL PRINCIPLES

1. Ownership of land: historical introduction

The terminology of English land law, and some of the concepts found in this area of law, are notoriously complicated. Much of this complexity can only be explained by reference to history. A detailed examination of the history of English land law is outside the scope of this project, but a few brief remarks may be appropriate.

The first point to note is that in English law it is technically incorrect to refer to any individual other than the King or Queen as the "owner" of land. As a direct consequence of the universal introduction (in 1066, following the Norman Conquest) of the so-called "feudal system" of land-holding, the King or Queen is, in theory, owner of all land; everyone else is merely a "tenant" in the feudal sense – one who holds land of the Crown in return for services (note that this use of the word "tenant" is distinct from its modern meaning – see section 2 below). Historically, there were a great many different types of feudal tenure, conventionally classified according to the type of service the tenant might be required to perform. The practical aspects of feudal tenure (including the tenant's obligation to provide services) had mostly disappeared by the 19th century, and the last trace of the distinction between the different types of tenure was abolished in 1922 (Law of Property Act 1922, s.128, Sch.12, para.1), but it remains true, as a matter of legal theory, that the most that a subject can own is an "estate" in land – an interest that is less extensive than the absolute ownership of the Crown. The only circumstances in which this has any practical consequences in the modern law are when an individual dies leaving no heirs who can inherit the land and having not made a will, and when an individual or company has become insolvent and the trustee in bankruptcy or company liquidator disclaims the estate: in such cases the land will "escheat" (i.e. revert back) to the Crown.

The second historical point relates to the terminology used to describe estates and other interests in land. Until the Judicature Acts 1873 and 1875, England had two separate and distinct court systems – the common law courts (principally the Court of King's/Queen's Bench and the Court of Common Pleas) which applied the rules of the common law, and

* University of Essex.

the Court of Chancery, which applied its own set of rules, the rules of equity. An estate in land, or an interest less than an estate in land, which was recognised by the common law courts in accordance with the common law rules would be described as a "legal estate" or a "legal interest", whereas an estate or interest recognised by the Court of Chancery in accordance with the rules of equity would be described as an "equitable estate" or an "equitable interest". The court systems were amalgamated in 1875, with the establishment of the Supreme Court of Judicature, but the two sets of rules were not amalgamated: all courts were to apply both the rules of the common law and the rules of equity (and in the case of conflict between the two sets of rules, the rules of equity were to prevail: Judicature Act 1873, s.25(11)). As a consequence of this, the distinction between legal and equitable estates and interests survived. It survives into the modern law, but now has a different basis, which is described in the following section.

2. Legal estates in land

English land law underwent radical chance in 1925. The Law of Property Act 1925 [LPA 1925] (one of a series of reforming acts which came into force on 1 January 1926) provided a new definition of "legal estates" and "legal interests" in land, which cut the terms free of their historical roots in the old common law courts. In the modern law, the only legal estates and legal interests which can exist are those which are listed in s.1 of the LPA 1925 – any other interest in land will be an equitable interest.

The two legal estates listed in s.1(1) LPA 1925 are:

1. The fee simple absolute in possession
2. The term of years absolute

The fee simple absolute in possession is the closest thing to absolute ownership of land in English law – it is often referred to as a "freehold estate" or "freehold ownership", and it is common (if technically inaccurate) for the holder of a fee simple estate to be described simply as the "owner" of a piece of land. The phrase "fee simple absolute in possession" is one which has a long history. It denotes an interest in land which is inheritable and will last for more than one lifetime (a "fee", as opposed to a life interest), which is free of any restriction on the class of people who may inherit the land (a fee "simple", as opposed to the old "fee tail" which was used in family settlements), which is free of conditions or limitations ("absolute", as opposed to "conditional" or "determinable"), and which will take effect immediately ("in possession", as opposed to "in reversion" or "in remainder"). In relation to this last phrase, it should be noted that "possession" in this context is not the same as "occupation" – the freehold owner does not lose his legal estate in land if he permits someone else to occupy the land (for example by granting a lease of the land to a tenant); this is an old rule of English law reiterated in s.205(1)(xix) LPA 1925, which provides that "possession" includes "receipt of rents and profits or the right to receive the same".

The second of the two legal estates recognised by the LPA 1925, the term of years absolute, is a "leasehold estate", often referred to as a "lease" or "tenancy". A leasehold estate will arise when the freehold owner of land gives another person or body the right to exclusive possession of the land for a period of time, usually (but not invariably) in return for a capital sum or the regular payment of rent. The freehold owner in such a relationship will be termed the "lessor" or "landlord", the person or body occupying the land the "lessee" or "tenant". Once again, this concept is much older than the 1925 legislation. The use of the phrase "term of years absolute" in the LPA 1925 is rather unhelpful: there is no requirement in English law that a lease must be for any particular duration, and a short-term lease for a matter of days, weeks or months may still be a valid "term of years" – s.205(1)(xxvii) LPA 1925 provides that a "term of years" "includes a term for less than a year, or for a year or years and a fraction of a year or from year to year". The word "absolute", as used in this context, is meaningless (or, at best, redundant). It certainly does not bear the same meaning as it does in the phrase "fee simple absolute", i.e. free from conditions and limitations; most leases will impose a large number of conditions on the tenant (not least the obligation to pay the agreed rent).

3. Creating and transferring legal estates

English law has strict formality requirements for the transfer and creation of estates in land. The basic rule is contained in s.52 LPA 1925 – all conveyances (i.e. formal transfers of land) "are void for the purpose of conveying or creating a legal estate unless made by deed". The definition of a "deed" is considered below, and it should be noted that there is an exception for short leases. But in practice, in the context both of residential property and commercial property, it is usual for there to be two separate documents (or sets of documents), a contract which records the agreement between the parties that a legal estate is to be transferred, and (some time later) a deed by which the transfer is effected. [In all cases of transfer of a freehold estate, and in the case of longer leases, there is now a further essential stage – the transfer must be registered; this is considered in section 4 below.] There are a number of reasons for the two-stage "contract and conveyance" procedure, but the most important one in the commercial context is that it gives the parties a considerable measure of security. Once the contract has been concluded in the appropriate form, the parties are, as is explained below, bound to proceed with the transaction, and can incur financial commitments (borrowing money to fund the purchase or to develop the property, for example) in the knowledge that the transfer will go ahead (or that they will be able to seek compensation if it does not).

In relation to contracts, the general rules of English law do not require that agreements between parties should be recorded in any particular form – for a contract to buy an item of personal property (property other than land) there is no requirement that the agreement should be in writing or that there should be any written evidence of the agreement. Contracts to transfer an estate in land (conventionally referred to as "estate contracts") form a major exception to these general rules, and the law imposes strict requirements. The rule originally contained in the LPA 1925 s.40 (which can be traced back to the Statute of Frauds 1677) was that a contract for the sale of land (or of any interest in land) could only be enforced if it was in writing, or if there was some written evidence of the contract which bore the signature of the party against whom action was brought. In some cases, a contract for the sale of land which did not meet these requirements might nonetheless be enforced through the equitable doctrine of "part performance": if one party had relied on the existence of an informal contract and had incurred loss as a result, he might be able to ask a court to enforce the contract. More recent legislation, the Law of Property (Miscellaneous Provisions) Act 1989 [LP(MP)A 1989], has imposed a stricter rule. Under s.2 LP(MP)A 1989, a "contract for the sale or other disposition of an interest in land can only be made in writing and only by incorporating all the terms which the parties have expressly agreed in one document or, where contracts are exchanged, in each" (s.2(1) LP(MP)A 1989). [The final clause of this section refers to the fact that it is usual for there to be "exchange of contracts", rather than one single contract – two identical copies of the contract are prepared; one is signed by the seller and one by the buyer, and, when the parties are ready to proceed, the two signed copies are exchanged.] The contract (or contracts) "must be signed by or on behalf of each party to the contract" (s.2(3) LP(MP)A 1989).

The changes introduced by s.2 LP(MP)A 1989 were highly significant. The old rule contained in s.40 LPA 1925 had, in essence, been a rule of evidence: contracts for the sale of land could be formal or informal, but the only evidence of such contracts that the courts would accept (save in cases where a valid claim of part performance had been made) was evidence in writing. The new rule is simple: it is no longer possible to have an informal contract to transfer an estate in land – an agreement which does not comply with the requirements of s.2 LP(MP)A 1989 will not be a contract. Inevitably, this means that there is no room for the doctrine of part performance to operate, though there may still be the possibility in rare cases of relying on other equitable doctrines, such as proprietary estoppel (see *Yaxley v Gotts* (2000)). Following the decision of the House of Lords in *Yeoman's Row Management Ltd v Cobbe* [2008], which is discussed in more detail later in this paper, it is clear that this doctrine has only limited scope for application in the commercial context. It may apply as between two parties to a "joint venture" purchase of property (as in *Yaxley v Gotts*, where one party had provided money to fund the purchase of property for redevelopment, and the other had provided labour to redevelop it in the expectation of receiving an interest), but it will not apply as between buyer and seller to give effect to an incomplete "gentleman's agreement".

The danger of section 2 is that it has the potential to be a "contract-breaker's charter". Suppose the parties have not included all the terms in one document, or have in some other way failed to comply with the requirements of the section. If one party wishes to change his mind, can he make use of this fact to avoid his obligations? The approach that the courts have taken to s.2 LP(MP)A 1989 has been purposive – they have looked at the mischief the Act was intended to solve, in an attempt to make sure that the Act cannot simply be used as an escape route by those who have entered into bargains which they have come to regret. The Act was clearly intended to increase certainty in property transactions – to ensure that the parties knew exactly what their obligations were, and that they did not incur legal liability on the basis of, for example, informal correspondence. Where the parties have in fact reached an agreement the principal terms of which are certain, the courts will be reluctant to deny legal force to that agreement because of a slight failure to comply with the letter of s.2 LP(MP)A 1989.

This purposive approach can clearly be seen in two of the earliest cases brought under this section of the LP(MP)A 1989, both involving "missing terms". In each case a party who wishes to escape from his obligations sought to argue that the contract did not contain all the terms agreed by the parties. The courts managed to avoid the strict operation of s.2 by construing the terms that were not included in the written contract as collateral contracts – separate agreements that fell outside the scope of section 2: *Record v. Bell* (1991) and *Tootal Clothing v. Guinea Properties Management* (1992).

In a similar purposive approach to the statute, though in a very different context, it is clear that in some cases interests in land can be affected by transactions which do not meet the strict requirements of s.2, simply because the transactions are not contracts "for the sale or other disposition of an interest in land". An early example occurred in *Spiro v. Glencrown Properties* (1991). One party had been granted an option to purchase a piece of land. He exercised his option in writing, but the other party (who wished to escape from the agreement) said that this was not enough to satisfy s.2 LP(MP)A 1989, because the document exercising the option had been signed by only one party. The court rejected this, and stated that it was sufficient if the agreement granting the option complied with s.2; the option could then be exercised unilaterally by the buyer. Another – and perhaps more useful – example of the same approach occurs in *Pitt v PHH Asset Management* (1994). In this case, a potential buyer of land had entered into a "lock-out" agreement with the seller: the seller agreed, in return for consideration, not to consider other offers for a specified period. The court held that the "lock-out" agreement was valid, and did not require to be in writing signed by both the parties, as it fell outside the scope of s.2. More recently, the courts have reached the same conclusion in *Nweze v Nwoko* (2004) about a compromise agreement, in which a property dispute between two parties was settled by, among other things, an agreement to place property on the market: this was valid even though it did not comply with the requirements of s.2. At times, a court's desire to hold parties to their agreements does some harm to the logic of the section: in another case, *Joyce v Rigolli* (2004), a boundary agreement (an agreement between the parties resolving a dispute as to the exact line of the boundary between their properties) was held to be outside s.2, even though on the facts it appeared that some land would change hands as a consequence of the agreement. The court's approach was avowedly purposive: "it is a well-established part of the court's role to see whether a situation has arisen in which the mischief against which Parliament has legislated does not apply or is outweighed by other policy considerations of the law, and if so, whether an acceptable way of dealing with that problem can be found" (Arden LJ).

Even allowing for the purposive approach, s.2 still provides pitfalls for the unwary: in *Chandler v Clark* (2002) a husband's letter releasing his interest in the former matrimonial home to his wife was not a valid contract, because the wife had not signed it – as a consequence, she could not rely on it. For another case in which the letter of s.2 was applied, see *Sharif v Sadiq* (2004): the claimant sought to argue in this case that his informal agreement to buy shop premises was "an agreement to exchange contracts for the sale of an interest in land", not a "contract for the sale or other disposition of an interest in land", and that it therefore fell outside the scope of the section (relying on the Court of Appeal's discussion of the compromise agreement in *Nweze v Nwoko*, above). The court rejected this claim, noting that "nothing was said in Nweze's case, which concerned an agreement to place property on the market, as to the application of s.2 to a case such as the present where A agrees with B that he will enter into a contract for a disposition of an interest in land to B"; in such a case, the formality requirements in s.2 must be observed.

In another judicial development, which occurred shortly after the first version of this paper was written, the House of Lords has imposed clear limits on the availability of the remedy of "proprietary estoppel" in the commercial context: *Yeoman's Row Management Ltd v Cobbe* [2008] UKHL 55 (judgment 30th July 2008). Proprietary estoppel is a remedy based on a general notion of unconscionability: at its simplest, a party who has made a representation on which the other party has relied to his detriment will be held to his representation. This had threatened to undermine the requirements of s.2 LP(MP)A 1989 by mimicking the old doctrine of "part performance". In *Yeoman's Row* one party sought to enforce an "agreement in principle" that property would be transferred to him for an agreed price, on the basis that he had expended considerable time, effort and money in securing planning permission for redevelopment (a necessary precondition of the transfer) and the other party had then changed her mind. The House of Lords held that there was no contract. There are repeated references in the judgment to the commercial background of the parties, and it is clear that the latitude that might have allowed in the residential context could not apply here:

> It would be an unusually unsophisticated negotiator who was not well aware that oral agreements relating to such an acquisition are by statute unenforceable... Mr Cobbe was an experienced property developer and Mrs Lisle-Mainwaring gives every impression of knowing her way around the negotiating table. Mr Cobbe did not spend his money and time on the planning application in the mistaken belief that the agreement was legally enforceable. He spent his money and time well aware that it was not. Mrs Lisle-Mainwaring did not encourage him in a belief that the second agreement was enforceable. She encouraged him in a belief that she would abide by it although it was not. Mr Cobbe's belief, or expectation, was always speculative. He knew she was not legally bound. He regarded her as bound "in honour" but that is an acknowledgment that she was not legally bound.
> [2008] UKHL 55 at [27]; Lord Scott.

This is an important decision in that it closes a potential loophole; a developer or investor can identify with certainty the point at which he undertakes legal obligations, and is unlikely to be trapped into a binding agreement at an earlier stage.

In the *Yeoman's Row* decision and elsewhere in property law, we can see the English courts drawing a distinction, not generally made explicit in the legislation (other than in the legislation which regulates leasehold tenancies), between commercial and domestic situations. In the domestic context the courts are much more likely to make equitable remedies available, and to take account of any perceived inequality of bargaining power. Where the parties are experienced in business matters, are negotiating at arm's length, and have access to the same level of legal advice, the courts will take a firmer line. The same distinction can be identified, for example, in the field of the definition of property interests: see case-law on the "lease/licence distinction" and recent decisions of the senior courts regarding co-owned property.

The legal consequence of the existence of a valid contract (or of a valid exchange of contracts) is simple: it is the point of no return. It is generally the case that estate contracts fall into the category of "specifically enforceable contracts" – if either party refuses to proceed with the transaction, the other party can request "specific performance", i.e. ask a court to order that the transfer should be completed. Although specific performance is technically a discretionary remedy, it will usually be preferred by the court to the award of damages – because each piece of land is unique, it is felt that the breach of a contract to transfer land, or to create a leasehold estate or other interest in land, cannot adequately be compensated by the award of a sum of money alone. An estate contract may also be enforceable against third parties, in situations in which the seller has transferred land to someone else, having previously entered into a contract to transfer it to the claimant, or to grant a lease to the claimant. The existence of an estate contract gives the claimant an equitable interest in the property which he can protect by registration (either by means of a notice in the register of the seller's title, in the case of registered land, or by recording a land charge against the name of the seller, if title to the land is unregistered – see section 4 below). If this has been done, then the contract is specifically enforceable against the third party, and the claimant is entitled to call for the freehold estate or a leasehold estate (as appropriate) to be transferred to him on the terms that he agreed with the previous owner.

A valid contract gives the purchaser substantial rights, but it does not give him a legal estate in land – as noted earlier, s.52 LPA 1925 requires a deed to be used for this. For many centuries, the requirements of English law were that a deed should be signed, sealed and delivered. The requirement of a seal on all deeds was centuries old, and dates back to the days before (near-)universal literacy, when an individual's seal would be the best proof of his consent to a transaction. In modern times it had become largely symbolic, and in many cases the "seal" was simply a small disc of red adhesive paper, or a pre-printed red disc at the foot of a standard-form document. The LP(MP)A 1989 removed the requirement that a seal should be used in all cases of deeds executed by individuals – instead, a deed must (a) make it clear on its face that it is intended to be a deed, and (b) be signed, witnessed and delivered (s.1 LP(MP)A 1989). Seals may still be used for some deeds executed by corporations.

The only significant exception to the requirement that a deed be used to transfer a legal estate relates to short leases. A valid lease may be created for a period not exceeding three years without any formality (s.54 LPA 1925), provided that it takes effect "in possession" (i.e. immediately) and that it is "at the best rent which can be reasonably obtained" – not only is a deed not necessary for such a lease to be created, but there need be no written evidence of it in any form, and a contract to create such a lease does not need to comply with the provisions of s.2 LP(MP)A 1989. A lease created in this way without any formality (termed a "parol lease") will still qualify as a legal estate. In practice, and especially in the commercial context, it is very rare for a lease to be created, even for a short period, without the use of written documents – although s.54 LPA 1925 ensures that parol leases may still be created, there are obvious problems of proof in the event of a dispute between landlord and tenant if none of the terms of their agreement are in writing. It should be noted that the exception to the formality requirements for short leases in s.54 LPA 925 only applies to the *creation* of such leases; if a legal leasehold interest is *assigned* (i.e. transferred in its entirety to a new tenant) then a deed must be used in all cases if the assignment is to be effective to transfer a legal estate in the land.

4. Registration of title

One of the principal aims of the 1925 legislation was to introduce universal registration of title – the notion that ownership of all land, and of interests in land, should be centrally recorded. This was not a new idea in 1925 – it can be traced back to the Royal Commission on Land Transfer and Registration in 1857, and the English system owes much to the so-called "Torrens scheme" first introduced in 1858 in Australia – but until 1925 registration of title in England had proceeded on a local and voluntary basis. The Land Registration Act 1925 [LRA 1925] sought to change this, but it was not to be an overnight change. The intention was that certain parts of the country would be designated as areas of "compulsory registration", and that when land changed hands (typically by sale, in the early stages of the move to universal registration) in such areas the new proprietor would be obliged to complete the transaction by registering his title to the land. It appears that the original aim of the draftsmen of the 1925 legislation was that all title to land should be recorded within a generation of the coming into force of the LRA 1925; this was not accomplished, and despite the fact that all parts of England and Wales have been areas of compulsory registration for some 20 years there is still some "unregistered land" to which the old rules apply. The LRA 1925 has now been repealed and replaced by the Land Registration Act 2002 [LRA 2002]; one of the objectives of the LRA 2002 is to speed up the process of land registration.

It is frequently said that three fundamental principles underlie the system of registration of title – the "mirror", "curtain" and "insurance" principles (though none of these terms is used in the legislation). The "mirror" principle suggests that the Land Register established by the LRA 1925 should be an accurate reflection of all aspects of ownership of the land: it should enable a purchaser to find out not only the extent of the land and the identity of the current freehold estate owner, but also the full range of benefits and burdens which affect the land. This principle has never been fully achieved, either under the LRA 1925 or the LRA 2002, because the English system of land registration (unlike its more absolute counterparts in some other common law countries) has always allowed for a category of interests (termed "overriding interests" in the LRA 1925) which are binding on a purchaser of land even though they have not been recorded on the Land Register. The list of such interests has been reduced by the LRA 2002, and the terminology has changed slightly (to "interests which override first registration" and "interests which override registered dispositions", Schedules 1 and 3 LRA 2002), but it should be noted that the existence of these interests, often referred to as the "crack in the mirror", means that a potential purchaser can never rely on the Land Register alone, but must always inspect the land carefully and make further enquiries of those who occupy it.

The "curtain" principle is chiefly relevant to domestic conveyancing, but it may also apply in a commercial context. It relates to the institution of the trust, the recognition of which was the principal achievement of the old Court of Chancery. The idea of the trust is that ownership of a legal estate in land can be separated from beneficial enjoyment (i.e. the right to enjoy the benefits) of that land: the legal owner may hold the land as a trustee, and others, the beneficiaries of the trust, may be entitled to occupy the land or to receive the profits from it. Trusts of land can be created expressly (by signed writing, s.53 LPA 1925), but they may also arise by implication (termed "resulting" or "constructive" trusts). A common example of an implied trust in the domestic context arises when one party acquires a freehold estate in land, but pays for the land with money supplied by someone else; if there is no evidence that the person supplying the money intended it to be a gift or a loan, then that person acquires an equitable interest in the land as the beneficiary under an implied trust. The intention of the LRA 1925 and the LRA 2002 is that the details of trusts of land should be hidden behind a metaphorical curtain: the prospective purchaser should be able to find out that a trust exists, but he need not concern himself with the details of that trust. If the purchaser knows that land is held on trust, then he must pay his purchase money to at least two trustees; this will have the effect of "overreaching" the beneficiaries' equitable interests, and turning them into interests in the proceeds of sale (s.2 LPA 1925).

The "insurance" principle is easily explained: the state guarantees the accuracy of registered title. If it transpires that there is a mistake on the Land Register, then state funds will be used to pay an indemnity to anyone who suffers loss as a result of the correction of that mistake. The *symbolic* importance of this state guarantee may be more important than its practical application: the Land Registry is very proud of its success rate, and the *Annual Report 2009/10* states that 98.98% of all registrations for that year were processed free of any error. Despite this impressive success rate, mistakes can happen – and in any event, as is noted below, the "insurance" principle does not only protect the purchaser of land from mistakes made by Land Registry staff.

When something has gone wrong and a mistake is discovered on the Register, schedule 4 of the LRA 2002 ("Alteration of the Register") sets out the procedure that will apply. Both the courts and the Registrar are given substantial powers to amend the Register to correct mistakes, bring the Register up to date, or to give effect to interests excepted from the effect of registration: Schedule 4, 2(1). But this wide power is qualified by a restriction (albeit not total) which has an obvious link to the concept of "legal certainty". When a proprietor is in possession of land and alteration would affect his title to it, no order may be made against him unless he has caused or substantially contributed to the mistake "by fraud or lack of proper care", or it would be "unjust for the alteration not to be made": Schedule 4, 3(2) and 6(2). There is a strong presumption that those who are in possession of land – who have of course paid for the right to be there in reliance on the Register – will be allowed to remain in possession.

The provisions regarding alteration of the Register form the background to the "insurance" principle; in the foreground are the provisions of Schedule 8 LRA 2002 regarding indemnities. Indemnities are payable where there has had to be "rectification" of the Register. Rectification is a subspecies of alteration, defined (Schedule 4(1)) as any alteration which both involves the correction of a mistake, and prejudicially affects the title of a registered proprietor. Indemnities are payable in cases of obvious administrative error – where the registry has lost documents, has supplied inaccurate replies to search requests and other types of negligence – but are not limited to this category; a person who buys property relying on forged documents may well receive an indemnity (provided that he exercised proper care at all times) when the forgery comes to light. The two principal cases where an indemnity will be paid are to a person who suffers loss "by reason of rectification of the register" (i.e. because the formal record is changed to correct a mistake), or to a person who suffers loss by reason of "a mistake whose correction would involve rectification of the register" (i.e. where there has been a mistake but no change in the formal record, typically because of the provisions noted above that limit the circumstances when the Register may be altered against a proprietor in possession).

The indemnity provisions, like the provisions of any insurance policy, do not relieve a person involved in property transactions from all obligations. An indemnity will not be paid if the claimant has caused the loss by his own "fraud" or "lack of proper care", and may be reduced if he has contributed to the loss in the same way, in proportion to his contribution. It also remains necessary to inspect the land carefully; if the Register is rectified to give effect to an "overriding interest", then no indemnity will be paid.

Both the indemnity provisions and the substantial restriction on rectification against a proprietor in possession are designed to maximise the certainty and security of property transactions. They do so, of course, at a cost to the state: the *Annual Report 2009/10* shows that a total of just over £7.7m. was paid (for 1011 claims) in that year. By far the largest proportion of this (63.6% of the total; £4.5m., for 53 claims) was paid in relation to cases of fraud and forgery. Unsurprisingly, the report also states that "We have introduced measures intended to counteract registration fraud". That said, the income generated by the registration system can easily bear this level of indemnity: the total fee income received in 2009/10 was £328.4m., so slightly less than 2.5% of income was returned to dissatisfied customers.

When title to a piece of land has been registered, then a potential purchaser will be able to obtain three sets of information. The Property Register provides a description of the property and lists any rights which attach to it (the benefit of a right of way over neighbouring land, for example). The Proprietorship Register states the name and address of the registered proprietor, and also states the nature of his title – there are a number of different categories which can exist here (absolute, qualified or possessory in the case of freehold title; absolute, good, qualified or possessory in the case of leasehold title), which depend on the evidence supplied to the Land Registry at the time the estate was registered. In the overwhelming majority of cases of freehold estates the Register will show "absolute" title; most leasehold estates will also be "absolute", but "good" leasehold title will exist when the leasehold title has been registered, but the freehold estate out of which it has been created has not itself been recorded on the Register. The Charges Register shows third party rights which adversely affect the land – the most common example of such a charge will arise when land has been mortgaged in return for a loan of money, either at the time of acquisition or at a later date. Third party interests which fall outside the categories of interests which override first registration and interests which override registered disposition must be protected by entry on the register of a restriction or notice – as noted in the previous section, an "estate contract" is one such interest.

When title to a piece of land has not previously been registered, then the old system of investigation of title in English law must be employed. The purchaser will need to check the title deeds – the formal documents (conveyances, mortgage deeds etc.) generated when land was transferred or when interests in land were created. The seller of property will need to show a good title to the land for a period of at least 15 years (s.23 Law of Property Act 1989). As with land the title to which is registered, the purchaser will also need to inspect the land and to make further enquiries of those who occupy it. The 1925 legislation also introduced a "half-way house" for unregistered land – the land charges system, under which the holders of certain types of commercial interest in unregistered land could protect their interests by entry on the Land Charges Register against the name of the estate owner. This system was originally contained in the Land Charges Act 1925, and is now to be found in the Land Charges Act 1972, which lists the interests which can qualify as land charges in s.2. The purchaser of unregistered land will accordingly also need to check the Land Charges Register against the name of the current owner of the legal estate, and against the names of all previous owners as disclosed by the title deeds, to establish if any land charges have been registered. As noted in the previous section, an "estate contract" is one such land charge (Class C(iv); s.2(4) LCA 1972).

When any registered title is transferred, it is necessary for the transaction to be completed by registration on the Land Register – the name of the new proprietor will be registered on the Proprietorship Register, and any new charges or other interests will be recorded as necessary. A great many dealings with previously unregistered land will also now need to be completed by registration. The LRA 2002 provides (s.4) a list of events which will trigger the requirement to register. All transfers of freehold estates by sale, gift or inheritance must now be completed by entry on the Land Register, and so must grants of leases for more than seven years, and assignments of leases with more than seven years left to run. The list of triggering events in the LRA 2002 is much more extensive than its equivalents in earlier legislation, and is intended to speed up the move to universal registration of title. Where registration of title is compulsory (i.e. if land is already registered, or if one of the triggering events in s.4 LRA 2002 has occurred), then any relevant transaction must be completed by registration within two months (though in practice it is common for the registrar to grant an extension to this period); if an application for registration is not made within this period, then the transaction "becomes void as regards the transfer, grant or creation of a legal estate" (s.7 LRA 2002).

5. Mortgages

In many commercial and domestic land transactions, the purchaser will borrow some or all of the purchase-price from a lender, and will grant the lender a mortgage over the land in return. The mortgaged land acts as security for the repayment of the loan; the lender (or mortgagee) will have a range of rights which he can exercise over the land if the borrower (or mortgagor) is unable to make the agreed repayments. This type of mortgage, known as an "acquisition mortgage" is the most common in English law, but it is equally possible for land to be mortgaged at any time after acquisition, if the estate owner needs to raise money for any purpose. A piece of land may be mortgaged more than once. Most mortgages are created by deed and qualify as legal interests in land, but it is also possible for a mortgage to be an equitable interest, most commonly when it has been created by signed writing but is not contained in a deed.

Detailed consideration of the English law of mortgages is beyond the scope of this paper, but it may be useful to give a brief note of the remedies available to a mortgage lender. If the borrower defaults on his repayments, then it is usual for the lender to exercise his right to possession of the mortgaged property (generally after obtaining a court order, though it is one of the many oddities of the English law of mortgages that in many cases the lender will have an *automatic* right to possession even before there has been any default). Possession is usually a prelude to the exercise of the power of sale – the circumstances in which the power of sale arises and becomes exercisable, and the obligations of the lender in relation to the proceeds of sale, are regulated by ss.101, 103 and 105 LPA 1925. In the commercial context, the lender may also appoint a receiver (s.101 LPA 1925). The old remedy of foreclosure, which extinguished the borrower's rights over his property and transferred the property absolutely to the lender, is only available by court order and is for all practical purposes obsolete. A mortgage is both the grant of an interest in land and a contract between the parties for repayment of a loan, and the proprietary remedies available to a lender do not exclude his contractual rights – if a lender takes possession of property and sells it but the proceeds of sale are not sufficient to discharge the borrower's debt, then the lender may in addition sue the borrower for breach of his covenant to repay.

Alan Moran*

COMMERCIAL LEASES IN ENGLISH LAW

1. The role of the lawyer

Lawyers in the English legal system who work in a law firm partnership (or, very rarely, as a sole practitioner) are called solicitors. They are subject to extensive and strict regulation. Before 2007, the solicitors' governing body, the Law Society, regulated the solicitors' profession. Since 2007, a new independent body called the Solicitors' Regulation Authority regulates the profession. The SRA has made the Solicitors' Code of Conduct which contains mandatory rules and guidance which all solicitors must follow. Firms are regulated in matters relating to accounts and care of clients' money, the provision of financial advice, relations with other lawyers, with clients, and with third parties. No solicitor may practise without a Practising Certificate.

Professional ethical standards under the Code of Conduct regulate dealings between lawyers so that one lawyer may not act in an unethical manner towards another. At the same time, the interests of the client are paramount. There are strict rules governing the relationship not only between lawyers but between the lawyer and his client and between the lawyer and a third party.

In this connection, it should be noted that in England, a sufficient level of professional indemnity insurance is compulsory; lawyers cannot practise without such insurance. Such compulsory insurance is by no means to be found in all European countries. The level of cover is objectively determined so that it is adequate to cover risk. Accordingly, if a client suffers loss because of the proven negligence of his lawyer, that loss will be wholly compensated by insurance.

Under Rule 3.07 of the Code of Conduct, the parties to a commercial lease (hereafter 'lease') must be separately represented. Of course, this is designed to avoid any conflict of interest. Not only the landlord and the tenant should have separate representation but also any surety and also any mortgagee. This contrasts with the civil code legal system in which a notary acts for both sides, and, to a degree, represents the state. This difference illustrates the fact that the English common law system is adversarial; it is up to each

* University of Essex.

party to secure for itself the best position it can gain. The outcome is therefore a balance of interests that both parties can accept, but market conditions may give one party a stronger bargaining position than the other. In contrast to a system which uses the Notary, parties in the common law system feel more involved and in control of the transaction.

It is the function of the landlord's lawyer to draft the lease. This is done by reference to a precedent which will either have been drafted by a specialist draftsman or taken from an encyclopaedia of precedents. Thus, the lawyer acting is not responsible for drafting the whole document but he must ensure that the precedent is adapted to reflect exactly the landlord's instructions. Lawyers work best when they have proper instructions and it is unlikely that the landlord personally will have drawn up the instructions. Instead, a chartered surveyor with expertise in the marketing of commercial leases will have consulted with the landlord and drawn up the instructions for the landlord's lawyer. The landlord's lawyer must not rely only on the instructions of the chartered surveyor but must check with his landlord client that the instructions he, the lawyer, has received do in fact fully reflect the landlord's intentions.

The landlord's lawyer will then draft the lease and send two copies to the tenant's lawyer. The tenant's lawyer will also have been sent a copy of the instructions drawn up by the landlord's chartered surveyor, and he must check with his tenant client that these instructions accurately reflect the agreement made between the tenant and the landlord. The tenant's lawyer must check the whole of the draft lease even if he is familiar with the precedent used because he cannot be sure where the precedent has been adapted, and, because of the adversarial nature of the system, the landlord's lawyer is under no duty to inform the tenant's lawyer what changes he has made to a familiar precedent. The tenant's lawyer must ensure that the draft lease goes no further in placing obligations upon the tenant than has been agreed in negotiations or which are commonly placed upon tenants.

The tenant's lawyer may make amendments to the draft lease, and it is for both lawyers to negotiate any amendments. When any amendments have been agreed, the lawyers may proceed to completion of the lease.

2. Overview of the English commercial lease

The modern English commercial lease is regarded very much as a contract which happens to concern land. The law takes the view that business people deal with contractual matters all the time and so need a minimum of regulation by the state which assumes that they (and their lawyers) can look after themselves and know what they are doing. It follows that, like contracts, the drafting of leases lacks any proscribed procedure and is almost entirely a matter of professional practice and expertise. Accordingly, certainty in leases (save to the extent that the state does impose regulation) depends on the expertise of the lawyers rather than something which is imposed by law. Since leases and certainty of their terms depend on lawyers' expertise, case law – the common law – has played a very significant part in providing certainty. In recent years, judges have often commented that certainty is essential in property matters, and case law reflects the drive towards providing certainty. Lease precedents are revised to reflect the opinions of judges. It has to be admitted that many cases arise, not because there is inherent uncertainty in the usual procedures for drafting leases but because the quality of drafting has not been of a high enough standard; this has been commented upon frequently by judges. Cases may also arise when directors and employees in companies attempt to perform legal tasks instead of instructing lawyers. In defence of lawyers, it must be said that their work in this area can be extremely complex and mistakes can occur when clients set tight time limits and engage in elaborate corporate re-structuring which often involves multiple lease transactions within a group of companies. With the availability of a wide range of standardised precedents for documents stored on computers, there is less excuse for those mistakes that lead to errors. There are packages available for computer checklists and diary prompts which can reduce the scope for error and overlooking of deadlines. If clients set reasonable timescales for the conduct of a transaction and lawyers' offices have procedures for the avoidance of errors, complete certainty can be assured. Case law should not cause us to forget that the vast majority of transactions are free of problems. The task of the lawyers is to ensure that their documentation reflects the guidance that judges give on the construction and interpretation of individual lease clauses. The extent of statutory regulation is mentioned below.

The English courts especially have shown flexibility and creativeness in not only treating leases as contracts but in applying principles of contract law to leases, for example, the contractual doctrine of repudiatory breach. This provides that where A and B are parties to a contract and A fails to perform his part of the contract, then B may say to A that he, B, regards the breach as evidence that A intended by that breach to repudiate the contract and be no longer bound by it; so, B can then say that he accepts that repudiation and treat the contract as terminated. This doctrine has been imported into the law of landlord and tenant as follows. Suppose A is the landlord, L, and B is the tenant T. L has an obligation under the lease to repair the premises let to T. L fails to repair. T complains. L does nothing. T is entitled to regard L's failure to repair as repudiatory breach and may stop paying rent, leave the premises and return the keys. Another example of the incorporation of contract law into the law of landlord and tenant would be the doctrine of rectification: where a mistake is proven to have been made in the lease document, one party may apply to the court for rectification of the lease. There common law rules (that is, rules devised by judges) which govern how rectification may be effected.

The perception of the lease as a contract means that the courts are willing to approach the construction of wording in a very pragmatic manner. Where there is a dispute as to the construction of some wording in a lease, the courts will apply the principle of business efficacy; if the disputed wording can be interpreted in a way which accords with business efficacy, then that is the construction which the courts will put upon the wording. This is called, 'the presumption of reality'. There are limits to this approach. The courts know that they cannot re-write the contract for the parties. In matters of construction, the question which must be asked is, 'what is meant by what the parties have said'; the courts cannot ask the question, 'what did the parties mean to say?'

In English law, it is essential that a lease has two features: these are exclusive possession and a definite term. 'Exclusive possession' means that the tenant has all the rights of an owner and may exclude from the premises everyone including the landlord except to the extent that the landlord has contracted for re-entry to the premises for specific and limited reasons, for example to view the state of repair of the premises. 'Definite term' means that the tenant's interest is for a fixed period of time such as five years. Until the end of the term, the landlord's interest in his land is called a 'reversion' because the premises will revert to the landlord at the end of the term free of the lease. This reversionary interest has value and can be dealt with by sale or mortgage.

During the term of the lease, the common law of contract governs the landlord and tenant relationship; in other words, relations are governed by the terms of the contract. In simple cases, the lease document may be very short; in complex development projects, the lease document will be long and of sufficient complexity to manage the complex nature of the situation. In all cases there are standardised ways of dealing with common matters. The main ones of these are:

- amount of rent
- payment of rent
- provision for increase of rent ('rent review'), usually only upwards
- responsibility for insurance
- payment of any service charge
- definition of the term
- definition of the premises, by means of a plan
- covenants:
  - restricting the use of the premises
  - restricting alterations
  - dealing with liability for repairs
  - restricting alienation (assigning, subletting, mortgaging)
- forfeiture (allowing the landlord to recover the premises where the tenant is in breach of covenant).

3. Formalities for creation of a lease

A lease of more than three years must be created by deed. Where the lease is short, that is, seven years or less, there are no requirements to register the lease. Instead, the lease is automatically binding on anyone dealing with the landlord's reversionary interest. Thus, where L lets to T and L then sells his land to B, then B is automatically bound by T's lease and cannot override it in any way. This gives complete security to T during the term of the lease. This protection is provided by the Land Registration Act 2002.

Where a lease is created for more than seven years, it must be registered at the Land Registry to be protected. The lease is substantively registered with its own title at the Land Registry and a cross reference to the landlord's title is made by the lease being noted on the landlord's title. This means it cannot be ignored by anyone dealing with the landlord's title. The English registration system includes a guarantee by the state of the registered title. It is impossible to avoid this state guarantee of title. In the very rare case that the Land Registry makes a mistake, any loss is covered by the 'insurance principle' which means that any party suffering loss by reason of a mistake by the Land Registry is compensated by the state.

4. Protecting the tenant

Where a tenant makes improvements to the premises, legislation (the Landlord and Tenant Act 1927) provides for compensation to be paid to the tenant by the landlord for those improvements. It was recognised, however, that what tenants really needed was security when the lease term ended, that is the ability to stay on in the premises after the termination of the contractual term. This is provided for by the Landlord and Tenant Act 1954, Part II. The Act provides that when a commercial lease which qualifies for protection under the Act (and most such leases do so qualify) comes to an end, the tenant may have 'security of tenure', that is, the tenant may have the right to continue occupying the premises and be granted a new lease. A notice procedure is provided which must be followed on the termination of the lease. Either the landlord or the tenant can initiate the procedure. However, the Act does specify certain limited grounds on which the landlord may, on proving those grounds to the court, resist a claim by the tenant for a new lease. Notwithstanding the provisions of the Act, it is possible under the Act for the parties to agree to contract out of the security of tenure provisions of the Act so that the tenant does not have this protection. But both parties must agree to this and the agreement must follow certain statutory formalities to be effective. In England, such 'contracting out' is very common and it is thought that between one quarter and one half of all commercial leases are contracted out of the 1954 Act. This ability to contract out does not appear to have any effect on the commercial property market or on the level of rent that can be charged. There are criteria under which a tenant who is obliged to leave premises may receive compensation for disturbance.

5. Change of parties during the lease – enforceability of obligations

As between the original parties to the lease, there is a clear and binding contractual relationship and each party is bound by his obligations under the lease. Subject to the alienation clause, the tenant may assign the residue of the term of his lease or otherwise deal with it. The landlord may deal with, usually by selling, his reversionary interest. The question that arises when either or both original parties to the lease have parted with their interest is, are the respective obligations under the lease binding between the successors in title to the original parties to the same extent? The basic answer is 'yes'. The answer a few years ago would have involved a study of a very complex and archaic system of common law. The situation was recognised to be in need of modernisation, and so there was enacted the Landlord and Tenant (Covenants) Act 1995. The essence of the Act is that when the tenant assigns his lease he is automatically freed from all obligations under it except for any pre-existing breaches of covenant and the new tenant takes on all the tenant's obligations. The landlord who assigns his interest must apply to the tenant for release from his obligations but where the tenant refuses the landlord may apply to the court for a declaration that the tenant is behaving unreasonably. The Act, however, provides that, as a condition of giving consent to an assignment, the landlord may require the outgoing tenant to guarantee the obligations of the incoming tenant but only that tenant and not any further assignee. Such an agreement is called an Authorised Guarantee Agreement; in practice these are usual.

6. Factors outside the lease

When advising a tenant or a landlord, the lawyer in England must have regard to those factors outside the lease which nevertheless have an impact on the parties, especially the tenant in his use of the premises. The most obvious of these factors are legislation relating to planning and to environmental protection, and to existing restrictions in the landlord's title. The use to which premises may be put is regulated by planning law in the form of delegated legislation. There are 'use classes' describing the variety of uses to which premises may be put and tenants must comply with these according to the designated class of the premises. There are also planning restrictions relating to alterations which may need planning permission depending on certain criteria. Where a landlord wishes to keep close control of the use of and alterations to premises, he may put a clause in the lease which prohibits the tenant from applying for planning permission, thereby effectively severely limiting what a tenant can do. Landlords have to keep in mind that the more restrictions they impose, the more this will have the effect of depressing the level of rent which can be charged.

Where a site is being developed which has been used previously, the legislation protecting the environment must be taken into account. The relevant legislation is the Environment Protection Act 1990. Thus, where, for example, a developer intends to use the site of a former steel works to build a shopping centre, there is much specialised work to be done in terms of 'remediation' which means cleaning the site of all possible hazards such a pollutants.

7. Problems

The area which most commonly causes problems is time limits. Date-sensitive matters are of two kinds: common law or contractual provisions in the lease itself, and statutory matters. Common law matters include time limits for the exercise of break clauses and options (in which time is of the essence), and the operation of rent review clauses (though this is much less common in recently drafted leases which take account of the very clear judgments given in recent years). Statutory time limits are found in legislation for title registration, security of tenure procedures, and taxation. Common law matters and, obviously, statutory matters are in themselves certain; all that is required is office procedures to ensure compliance with time limits.

Problems may be caused by clauses which are drafted in a way which makes their meaning ambiguous. Current cases tend to arise from leases drafted some years ago; case law has provided a great deal of guidance on the interpretation of clauses, and current precedents should have been drafted to avoid ambiguity. In the interests of clarity of language (as well as of seeking a fair balance between the concerns of landlords and tenants), standard form lease documents have been drafted by several organisations including the Law Society with the Royal Institution of Chartered Surveyors, and the British Property Federation (which represents landlords) with the British Retail Consortium (which represents the largest group of tenants).

8. Providing certainty

Certainty has also been enhanced by two Codes of Practice. First, there is 'Commercial Property Leases in England and Wales – Code of Practice (2007)'. This is voluntary but its use is common by many leading property companies and City firms of solicitors. Secondly, standard forms of commercial property enquiries have been drawn up by The London Property Support Lawyers Group, and these forms are is wide use.

9. Statutory regulation providing certainty

Statute regulates the following matters: formalities for execution; by whom and against whom lease covenants may be enforced; security of tenure; the insolvency of parties; certain details regarding the operation of some covenants (such as repairs, assignment, and user) in order to prevent abuse; the taxation of leases and their assignment; the registration of some leases and dealings with them, and mortgages of them.

Other legislation affects commercial leases, especially planning and environmental law.

Certainty has been enhanced by the updating and improvement of earlier legislation. There has recently been a revision of the Landlord and Tenant Act 1954 Part II, which regulates security of tenure, and of the Land Registration Act 1925 has been entirely replaced by the Land Registration Act 2002. Among many things, recent amendment of the LRA 2002 now makes clear plans obligatory for leases. There is other legislation and regulation which relates to the confidence clients can have in their lawyers and the procedures they must follow; these cover such matters as the prevention of money laundering and the independent investigation of complaints against lawyers by the Solicitors Regulation Authority. It should be noted that in the English legal system, there is no state procedure for informing lawyers of changes in the law, either statute or case law. Lawyers make use of commercial organisations which provide updating services; such services provide daily updates in any chosen area of law. Larger firms also employ researchers whose function is to ensure that all lawyers in the firm are notified of developments and changes in the law.

I would repeat what I mentioned in an earlier paper, that in the jurisdiction of England & Wales, solicitors must have adequate professional indemnity insurance and in general parties to a lease must be separately advised so that conflicts of interest are avoided.

10. Conclusion

It is said by commentators in England that the law relating to commercial leases works very well. The common law developed over more than five hundred years and has been only slightly amended by legislation, most notably by the Landlord and Tenant (Covenants) Act 1995. The Landlord and Tenant Act 1954 Part II is said to have worked very well and has been only slightly amended recently and then largely in terms of procedure. The rules for the professional conduct of lawyers, compulsory professional indemnity insurance for lawyers, the state guarantee of title, the efficiency of the Land Registry, and the impartiality and integrity of the courts are recognised as providing a system in which parties to transactions can repose trust and confidence. Such factors are known to play a part in the decision of overseas investors (from, for example, Russia and the Middle East) to choose to invest in property in London. It has to be admitted, as already mentioned, that a great deal of litigation is generated only by weakness in the drafting of leases or by parties taking wrong steps. In any event, it is now recognised that litigation ought to be avoided whenever possible and a recent feature of the English legal system is the use of 'Alternative Dispute Resolution' and lawyers may be criticised if they fail to advise their clients to make use of ADR. It is also the case that only a tiny fraction of all legal matters in which argument arises result in litigation.

To sum up, if lawyers draft lease documentation correctly, or use standard documentation (properly adapted for the matter in hand), and if they have office procedures for the proper conduct of transactions, complete certainty is achievable, and is today widely achieved. The English legal system is characterised by freedom and flexibility on the one hand, and by certainty and security on the other.

PART III

MEASURING LEGAL CERTAINTY

Jean-Sylvestre
Bergé*

INTRODUCTORY REMARKS ON LEGAL SECURITY: THE APPROACH OF FRENCH AND EUROPEAN LAW**

In everyday language, "legal security" refers to the **supposed stability and predictability of legal solutions**. Law is there to steer or, more modestly, to accompany the action of institutions and individuals functioning or living in society. Among its objectives[1] is the definition of a general framework that is strong enough to allow actors to know in advance what they are allowed or not allowed to do.

In law, and in particular in French law, which is strongly influenced by European integration (COE – UE)[2], legal security can have two major benefits:

- It can have the value of a "legal principle", in which case we talk of the "principle of legal security"; here, legal security plays an extremely prominent prescriptive role: as we shall see, it serves to maintain existing legal systems and encourages the development of new ones;
- It is also a description tool (naturally, one that is not without a prescriptive dimension even if, in this case, its role is less prominent), in the sense that it sets out to examine the content of the rule of law with regard to the security that it is likely, or unlikely, to offer to those to whom it applies.

These two meanings of legal security, which are mutually complementary, deserve closer attention if they are likely to apply to the working hypothesis chosen by this research programme: real estate transactions.

* Université de Paris Ouest Nanterre La Défense, CEJEC

** This brief presentation complements work carried out on the concept of Legal Certainty by our colleague Youssef Farah, Professor at the University of Essex.

1 P. Roubier defined three such objectives: legal security, justice and social progress, in *Théorie générale du droit*, Sirey, 1951, p. 317.

2 In France, various works have focused on legal security recently. Among the numerous bibliographic references given, we can notably point out the excellent book coordinated by L. Boy, J.-B. Root and F. Siiriainen, *Securité juridique et droit économique*, ed. Larcier 2008.

1. Legal security: a prescription tool

1.1. Prescribing to establish the basis for the development of new legal systems: the European example

Here, the example of the European Union can be taken, showing how the "framework principle" of legal security – which covers a very large number of sub-principles (acquired rights, predictability of solutions, non-retroactivity, public nature of acts, legitimate confidence, etc.) – has been used from a very early stage by the Court of Justice (ECJ, April 6, 1962, Bosch, no. 13/61) to oversee the EU's standard-setting activity.

In a comparable manner, see also the jurisprudence of the ECHR (ECHR, June 13, 1979, Marckx v. Belgium).

Here, legal security plays a cardinal role. It supports the emergence of a European legal model (EU or COE) which, very early on, sought to establish itself based on a principle of legality or "community of law".

1.2. Prescribing to preserve the permanence of existing legal systems: the example of France taken in the European context

The affirmation of a general principle of European law in terms of legal security has had repercussions on the national legal systems of the Member States.

Insofar as France is concerned, we know:

- that the *Conseil constitutionnel* (Constitutional Council), even if it refuses to name it as such or to establish it as a principle, has made legal security one of the mainsprings for controlling legislative activity (see, on the subject of the understandability of law, in particular French law, its jurisprudence initiated in 1988; see more recently, e.g. Dec. 2005–530 of 29 Dec. 2005);
- that the *Cour de cassation* (Court of Cassation) has referred to it very regularly since 2004 (see, for the first judgements: Civ. 2, 8 July 2004 (2 judgements), Radio France and Generali; Soc. 17 dec. 2004, Samse);
- that the *Conseil d'Etat* (Council of State) established, from 2006 onwards (decision KPMG, 24 March 2006), the importance of "grounds for legal security" in the control of the State's regulatory activity (see more recently, e.g. CE, 25 June 2007, req. 304888).

Here, legal security appears as a means of maintaining the predictable and stable character of the solutions defined by the French national legal system. It has not, as with European law, been concerned with establishing a new legal system again, but rather with preserving the sustainability of a system which some consider as being threatened by an increasing level of instability and legislative or regulatory inflation.

1.3. *A few possible applications in the field of real estate transactions*

These different precedential statements of legal security may come to be applied in the field of real estate transactions, in particular in terms of:

- controlling the application of new rules (legislative or regulatory) over time, especially when they are intended to be applied to current contractual situations (transactions of sale or real estate loans in progress);
- limiting the effects in time of sudden changes in the case law, especially those implemented by ordinary courts for real estate law or credit;
- controlling the understandability of the legislative and regulatory texts applicable in these different areas.

Examples of application to these various domains will need to be developed.

2. Legal security: a description tool

2.1. *Describing to ascertain the ability of the rule of law to provide a certain degree of legal security*

When taken from an angle that is more descriptive than prescriptive[3], legal security can be used as a tool for evaluating the stability and predictability of the legal rules applicable to a given area.

It can notably be used to:

- identify the legal techniques which, within a given legal system, serve to ensure greater legal security,
- compare the respective efficiency of legal systems that are distinct from one another … especially in the context of the law applicable to real estate transactions.

2.2. *Legal security and legal technique*

As a general rule, French lawyers (perhaps unlike their English counterparts, see the speech by Y. Farah) working in the field of contract law – in particular civil law lawyers – do not give a precise meaning to the concept of "legal security".[4] In fact, this expression cannot be found in the index of reference books (summaries or treatises). At best, legal security appears as a notion with a of broad scope of application: legal security in terms of contract law is inseparable from legal security in terms of law in general. Any rule of law (e.g. on the absence of consent, the definition of the cause, the setting of the price,

3 …these two aspects are often inseparable one from the other.

4 Except, of course, on the issues already mentioned in §1 concerning the understandability of legal texts or, especially, the application over time of the law, of statutory instruments and of jurisprudence, including contractual situations in progress.

etc.) can thus be a pretext for an analysis in terms of "legal security". This pretext is often deemed unnecessary and, as a result, any explicit references to the concept remain rare.

In the French context, however, contractual matters provide a hypothesis where legal security is able to take on more concrete meaning. Here, we are thinking in particular about long-term contracts for which the passage of time may be a source of insecurity. Lawyers are led to reflect on the development of techniques – essentially contractual – intended to "secure" their transaction (e.g. a hardship clause), especially when the rule of law prohibits the judge, as is the case in French civil and commercial law (but there are many moderations to the rule), from modifying the contract unilaterally subsequent to a change of circumstances.

2.3. Legal security and legal comparison

Finally, legal security can serve as a yardstick when comparing different legal systems. In fact, herein lies the purpose of this research programme, dedicated to the modelling of legal security in terms of real estate transactions.

The descriptive aspect of this undertaking often badly conceals a profoundly prescriptive approach that tends to uphold the superiority of one system of law over another. Here, we can find the well-known discussions (Civil Law versus Common Law) – often polemical and of limited scientific value – that have surrounded the work of the World Bank (*Doing Business* reports).

To try to avoid falling into this trap, it might be a good idea to begin to agree on the actual meaning of "legal security" which, as we have seen in the French and European context:

- sometimes comes across as a "principle" in the doctrine and application of the rule of law;
- sometimes infers legal techniques intended to "secure" transactions;
- sometimes harks back to the commonly held – but also very vague – idea according to which legal security is nothing other than the ability of the rule of law to define stable and predictable solutions.

For our research, we believe it is essential to clarify the meaning to be given to this expression; this meaning may vary within the same legal system and, *a fortiori*, from one legal system to another.

Philippe Frouté*

AN ASSESSMENT OF THEORETICAL PROPOSALS TO DEAL WITH HETEROGENEOUS SMALL SAMPLES

The studies we conducted rapidly faced a big issue. Was it possible to make reliable quantified comparisons of differences in performance between notaries and non notaries legal systems using heterogeneous small samples? The underlying issues at stake concern different levels.

The first one is related with the cost of data collection. Indeed, to be relevant the traditional quantitative methods would work on panel data but require collecting detailed data for at least thirty individuals per country. This means having sufficiently standardized the methodology, but the previous chapters of this book show that this approach may be too simplistic and that it requires a very important preliminary work to comprehensively understand the legal systems. It is time and money consuming. In addition, standardizing data collection is not an easy task. Hence, it is necessary to achieve a trade-off between two conflicting objectives: defining sufficiently harmonised data to enable comparisons to be meaningful – comparability criterion – and defining data that are sufficiently representative of local conditions – representativeness criterion –. Then comes the actual step of collecting a sample whose size is sufficient enough.

The second issue is a practical one and relates to the statistical treatment of data. Indeed, working on small samples implies that the statistical properties necessary for using the usual estimators that are based on the central limit theorem are not satisfied. Traditional inferences used to assess the magnitude of the observed effects cannot be performed rigorously. We must therefore implement alternative methodologies.

We were not the only researchers facing these challenges. They often arise in public policy analysis when defining targeted measures is required. Fine tuning supposes to dispose of disaggregated information at an appropriate level. The institution which has developed the most such approach is the World Bank, particularly in the context of programs destined to diminish poverty. Notably, the Millennium Declaration adopted by the member countries of the United Nations in 2000 that called for the reduction of poverty by half in a worldwide scale by the year 2015.

* Assistant Professor in Economics. University Paris-Est Créteil. Faculty of Administration and International Trade. Codirector of the university diploma in International Political Science. Researcher at the Largotec.

The methodology developed by researchers at the World Bank belongs to the so-called small area estimations methodologies. It consists in fitting statistical models in order to be able to conduct statistical analysis for areas where the sample size of the survey data is not sufficient for generating accurate estimates.

Another example is the inclusion of heterogeneity in small samples. Innovative methodologies have been used to identify differences in institutional behaviour facing common contexts, particularly in the context of the economic crisis. The methodology changes the focus of the econometric analysis that is usually performed from the average people to consider different quantiles of the distribution. The methodology used is that of quantile regressions.

In this section I will present a critical analysis of these different methodologies: small area estimations and quantile regressions, in connection with the issue of conducting a comparative quantitative study of legal certainty. I will also present two examples of empirical research made using each of them. I will conclude by discussing the relevance of these methodologies to deal with the notion of legal certainty.

1. Small area estimations techniques

Nowadays, the main user of small area estimations techniques is the World Bank. The implementation of those statistical techniques is mainly driven by the monitoring of the Millennium development goals established by the United Nation in 2000. These techniques consist in generating estimates by fitting an econometric model to the dependent variable by using surveys and census data. They have been developed by renowned researchers such as You, Rao or Elbers and are still continue to give rise to methodological improvements.[1]

The first part of this section will present the methodological issues of these statistical techniques. The second part will present the results of one study using them for studying poverty in the Philippines. This section will end by discussing the relevance of using the small area estimation techniques in the case of international comparisons on legal certainty.

1.1. Methodological aspects

The best document to be introduced with the small area estimations methodology is the book from Rao entitled *Small Area Estimation* which has been published in 2003. In this book, Rao proposes a survey of the different possible methodologies.

The first category of model is called the **BLUP methodology**. BLUP means Best Linear Unbiased Prediction. Indeed, the BLUP methodology provides with the best estimates in a statistical sense of the notion, it means that amongst the linear and unbiased estimates, the BLUP estimates have the minimum mean square error. The predictions are linear because they are linear function of the data. Finally, they are

1 For instance, theses continue to be prepared on the issue: Isidro Marissa [2010], Intercensal updating of small areas estimates, PHD thesis in statistics, Massey University, Palmerston North, New Zealand.

unbiased because the estimate expected value is equal to the average value of the quantity being estimated.

The methodology is rather straightforward. It combines data gathered at a subsample level with data gathered at the sample or the population level. The idea is to use auxiliary variables available both at the survey and the census level to estimate a model explaining the dependent variable at the subsample level thanks to data collected at the census level. Assuming then that the relationship holds in the population as a whole, the methodology can predict missing dependent variable thanks only to census data.

If the population size of the small areas is sufficiently large, the use of the BLUP methodology can provide an estimate of the small area means as long as the sample data and the quantity into question fulfil the assumption of following the underlying chosen population model.

A more empirical view of the BLUP methodology is the EBLUP model. E stands for empirical. **EBLUP methodology** consists in replacing unknown's variance components by their estimates. On the one hand, it renders the result more dependent on the collected data, but in the other hand it makes it less dependent on *ad hoc* assumptions.

As explained by Rao other methodologies can be used, such as **Empirical Bayes** or **Hierarchical Bayes**. Statisticians have shown that some specification can make them similar to the EBLUP methodology. In practice, the EBLUP methodology is often preferred because it is simpler to use. Their main drawback is the necessity, especially in the case of the Hierarchical Bayes, to postulate an underlying assumption of the prior distribution in order to run the Bayesian process. Hence the results are conditional to this hypothesis.

Refinements of the methodologies have been made. An important question within this strand of comparative analysis is to respect an homogeneity hypothesis within the size of the different considered samples. Indeed, the result can be blurred if the sample size of a given area or country is very different from the others. That is why methodologies dealing with those differences have been implemented. They give the methodology the possibility to account for the weights of the different surveys. In a statistical sense of the notion those model are said to be design consistent (Isaki and Fuller, 1982, You and Rao 2002).

EBLUP models that take into account the survey weights in the estimation process are called **Pseudo-EBLUP.** A specific category of Pseudo-EBLUP has been developed by You and al. (2003). They have proposed an **Iterative Weighted Estimating Equation (IWEE)**, to include the possibility of difference sample sizes within the estimation of those components.

A second category of models have been developed to circumvent the linearity assumption of the modelling framework based on the BLUP approach of the small area estimation models. Those models have been developed by Elbers, Lanjouw and Lanjouw in the beginning of the 2000ies. Their methodology is known as the **ELL model**. It implements non linear estimates of parameters.

Recent works have complemented their approach by dealing with the issue of the simultaneity between the date of the sample survey and the date of the census. Indeed, using all those estimates to assess the dependent variable value outside of the year census is problematic because the estimates are computed assuming that the relationship exhibited during the census year is still relevant. A methodology coping with this issue has been developed by Isidro in 2010. It is called the **Extend Structure Preserving Estimation (ESPREE)** method, a methodology based on categorical data analysis.

Thus, the small area estimations field of statistics is still a promising on-going field of research. In the next paragraph, we will present the results on an analysis made using the ELL methodology in the case of the Philippines in 2005. The methodology has been implemented by the Philippines National Coordination Board in order to map poverty at the local level. The same kind of methodology has also been implemented in several low income countries as Thailand, Cambodia, Bangladesh and Vietnam, but also in more developed countries such as Brazil and South Africa. It the context of assessing legal certainty, one could think to use this methodology to assess particular laws in the context of the existence of common general principles.

1.2. The ELL approach

In this paragraph, I will present the result of an analysis conducted in the Philippines to address the issue of poverty at the local level in 2005.

The authors of the report have estimated per capita income and per capita expenditure at the barangay level.[2] They possessed direct estimates of these variables from sample survey data at the households' level. Hence those data lack of completeness. Indeed, they did not possess those estimates for all the barangays. In their study they used the ELL methodology to benefit from census data that were exhaustive to build more accurate estimates of poverty at the Philippines barangay level. The idea was to use auxiliary variables available both at the survey and the census level to estimate a model explaining per capita income or per capita expenditure at the barangay level thanks to data collected at the census level. Assuming then that the relationship held in the population as a whole, they have predicted missing per capita income or per capita expenditure thanks only to census data.

The original Elbers et al. procedure involved fitting the survey data using a two stage least squares procedure (Elbers et al., 2003). They also considered an alternative method (e.g. Skinner et al., 1989), which allows better incorporation of the sample survey weighting. They also used bootstrapping techniques to improve the fit of their model.

To run their study they gathered three set of data. The first one was the Family Income and Expenditure Survey conducted every three years by the National Statistics Office (NSO) of the Philippines. This survey collects information on household income, expenditure and consumption in addition to socio-demographic characteristics.

2 According to the authors, in 2000, the Philippines was composed of 79 provinces, which were grouped into 16 regions. Provinces are composed of municipalities, which are themselves divided into smaller units called barangays. Each barangay can be designated as urban or rural, with rural barangays corresponding to villages. Approximately 50 percent of the population lives in rural barangays.

The second survey is the Labour Force Survey, which collect data on the demographic and socioeconomic characteristics of the population over 15 years old.

Finally they considered the 2000 Census of Population and Housing which was the 11th national census conducted by the NSO. This full census is conducted every 10 years, with a Census of Population at 5-year intervals.

Their result is twofold. First, they produced small-area estimates of poverty in the Philippines at provincial and municipal levels, both from an expenditure-based and an income-based measure. Second they achieved this result thanks to a single predictive model for the whole country, instead of assessing at least 16 different models for the 16 regions.

In addition, this approach allows to achieve interesting results. Indeed, it allows to account for the spatial heterogeneity at a very disaggregated level. For example, it is used to distinguish a noticeable difference between the north and south of the archipelago in terms of wealth distribution.

This study shows (see the following map) that even northern areas close to the capital, Manila, are poor. Similarly in the southern part of the archipelago, near the city of Davao, there are areas with high-income enclaves next to clusters of disadvantaged areas.

This kind of mapping is used to design targeted programs destined to implement public policies. In the next paragraph I will discuss the relevance of this kind of methodology to deal with the issue of a quantitative comparison of legal certainty.

1.3. Small area estimations and legal certainty

Small area estimations techniques have clear advantages in the sense that they enable to cope with the absence of data. Indeed, following the ELL approach one can compute the missing ones thanks to the two steps approach.

Nevertheless, this advantage is also a major drawback that is itself twofold. Indeed, the methodology relies on the existence of a kind of meta-model defined at the population level. Indeed the missing data are computed as if each subsample variable was following this structural model. It is as if there exist structural components of legal certainty that were independent from the origin of the legal system. Or it is exactly what we wanted to test and what we have described in our legal analysis.

Hence, the two sides of the drawback are the following ones. First, the use of small area estimations techniques reduces the heterogeneity of the data because of the assumption of the existence of an underlying common model. Second, this underlying model makes the small area estimations a normative approach because the computation of the missing value is made following this model. It may appear as a constraint placed on the data.

Other methodologies may enable to tackle these issues. We will present one of them in the following section.

Graph. Poverty map in the Philippines

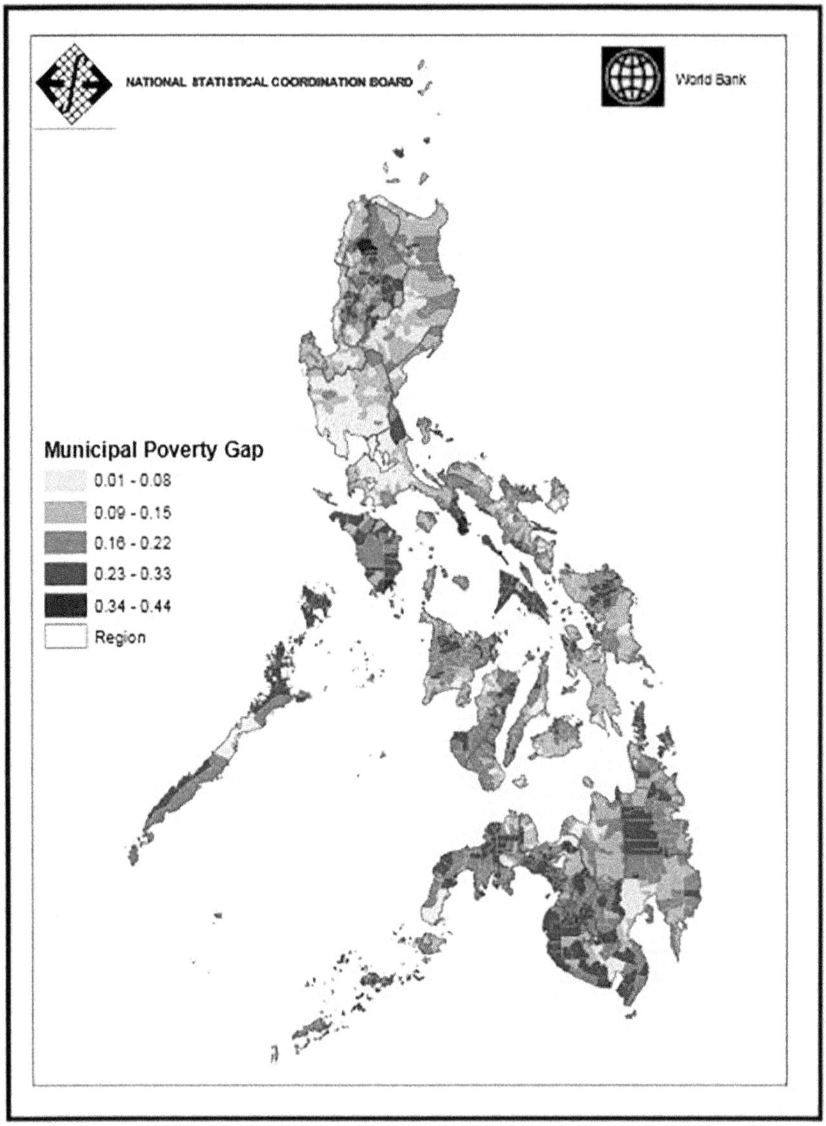

Source: NSCB (2005), Estimation of the local poverty in the Philippines, p. 61.

2. Quantile regressions

Small area estimations are not used to study empirically the issue of legal certainty. The majority of the current empirical literature on the notion is based on cross-section data, and on Ordinary Least Square, Instrumental Variables (IV) regressions and panel methods. The relevance of those methodologies is highly dependent on the number of observations especially when dealing with international comparisons. Another drawback is the fact that they assume parameter homogeneity. However, assuming homogeneous elasticities across countries and legal systems could lead to an over-fitting of conclusions based on the global population of economies to a particular subset of interest. Said differently, an empirical regularity found may differ in its relevance for certain subsets of countries if there is a heterogeneity bias underlying the data. This criticism joins the previous one made against the small area estimation methodology. By assuming a common underlying model, small area estimations prevent elasticities from being different between countries or between regions.

In our investigation, we propose the use of quantile regressions in order to improve upon the usual techniques by uncovering patterns in which the effect of a given variable, given the other determinants of legal certainty, could vary across countries.

The first paragraph will present the quantile regression methodology. The second will present the results of a study using quantile regressions. We will conclude by discussing the opportunity of using the quantile regressions methodology to address the issue of legal certainty.

2.1. *Methodological aspects*

Consider the linear model:

$$Y_{it} = X'_{it}\beta + v_{it} \tag{1}$$

where Y is the dependent variable and X is a vector of explanatory variables. The essential feature of a regression analysis is to examine the manner in which a set of explanatory variables affects the conditional distribution of a dependent variable. In the classical econometric techniques (OLS, IV, GMM, and GLS)[3], the component around which the dependent variable randomly fluctuates is the conditional mean $E[Y / X,\beta]$. However, unlike the classical approach, which amounts to estimating the conditional mean of the conditional distribution of Y, the quantile estimator is employed on different quantiles of the conditional distribution.[4]

Let $F(y)$ be the cumulated distribution function of Y. The θth quantile of Y is defined as the smallest y satisfying $F(y) \geq \theta$. In a regression context, it can be shown that finding θ amounts to obtaining the following estimator of β:

$$\hat{\beta}_\theta = \arg\min_{\beta_\theta} \left\{\sum_{i=1}^{T} H_\theta(v_{it})\right\},\ H_\theta(v_{it}) = \theta v_{it}^{+} + (1-\theta)v_{it}^{-} \tag{2}$$

where v_{it}^{+} is the vector of residuals with positive values and 0 otherwise, v_{it}^{-} is the vector of negative residuals and 0 otherwise. Therefore, we have as many estimators of β (and quantile regression estimates β) as values of $\theta \in (0,1)$ by changing the "representative" individual. The latter can be the mean (as in OLS), the median (θ = 0,5) or any other quantile. As θ can vary while considering all the individuals of the sample, we have a

3 GMM is the Generalized Method of Moments estimation; GLS is the Generalized Least Squares estimation.

4 Quantile regressions have been introduced by Koenker and Bassett (1978).

better image of the entire distribution conditional on the studied quantile. This approach possesses a double benefit:

- It enables to consider the heterogeneity of the sample and not to reduce it by focusing exclusively on the mean variable.
- As all the individuals of the sample are simultaneously considered whatever the quantile we are working on, this approach is useful to deal with small samples without having to split them further into smaller groups.

Concerning the econometrics issue, Koenker and Bassett (1978) have derived asymptotic normality results for the quantile regression and showed that:

$$\sqrt{T}\left(\hat{\beta}_\theta - \beta_\theta\right) \approx N\left(0,\, \theta(1-\theta)s(\theta)^2 J^{-1}\right) \tag{3}$$

$$J = \lim_{T\to\infty}\left(X'X/T\right) \tag{4}$$

$$s(\theta) = 1/f\left(F^{-1}(\theta)\right) \tag{5}$$

While the estimation of β is quite simple and requires the use of simplex algorithms (see D'Orey and Koenker (1987)), the estimate of the residual variance and the standard error of the estimated parameters is more complicated, since it requires the estimation of the unknown probability distribution function of y and its derivative. The latter is necessary to estimate the quantile density function $s(\theta)$, also called the sparsity function. Computation of the coefficient covariance matrices is an important part of quantile regression analysis and various approaches are available: bootstrap re-sampling methods, direct methods based on Siddiqui difference coefficients and kernel density (see Koenker and Bassett (1982), and Koenker (1994)). Hence, all the usual test statistics have to be computed according to the appropriate approach.

In the next paragraph I will present the main results of an analysis using the quantile regression methodology in the case of borrowing behaviour for the French regions.

2.2. Assessing behaviours' heterogeneity with quantile regression analysis

In France, local budgets must satisfy a Golden Rule. Local governments' accountability in France distinguishes between current expenditure and investment expenditure. Contrary to the central State budget, the Golden Rule imposes that each "section" (current and investment) of the budget has to be balanced and that borrowing has to be used for balancing the investment section. Thus, for a given level of investment and a given level of grants from the State budget, the need to balance the investment section forces local administrations to use their self-financing (e.g. current receipts in excess of current expenditure) or to borrow.

Borrowing is exclusively aimed at financing investment[5] (equipment expenditure and purchase of durable goods). Financial costs, including interest payments, are

5 Borrowing needs not be explicitly assigned to one or more investment transactions specifically designated in the contract. They can be aggregated and correspond to the overall need for financing the investment section.

considered as current expenditure (this assignment is a requirement from the Golden Rule which aims at achieving a good intertemporal management: the burden of the loan which defers the cost of funding on future generations must be covered by current resources). Another function of borrowing is to act as an adjustment variable depending upon the rooms for manoeuvre of local governments. The latter depend upon two factors: the amount of transfers from the State budget and local tax revenues. The amount of indebtedness depends on the existing stock of debt and its related mortgage.

Hence, at least intuitively, the Golden rule should normalize borrowing behaviours. Nevertheless, the authors provide empirical evidence of the heterogeneous borrowing behaviours of the French regions, despite the Golden rule.

To this end, they use a quantile regression analysis covering the period from 1999 to 2007 for the 22 metropolitan regions, which is a panel with a small number of data.

The authors investigate the usual determinants of borrowing: Investment needs, past borrowing, past debt levels, self-financing capacities and the level of interest rates as a proxy for credit cost. By considering different quantiles, the authors want to look if borrowing behaviour is constrained and homogenous or, on the contrary, if the different regions are adopting heterogeneous behaviour. They find that French regions borrowing behaviours vary between regions (see the following table). For instance, big borrowers ($\theta = 0.75$), are more sensitive to past debt level (coefficient equal to –2.86) in comparison with small borrowers ($\theta = 0.25$), (coefficient equal to –1.65) and average borrowers ($\theta = 0.5$), (coefficient equal to –1.39). Another interesting feature is that the coefficient developments are not linear.

Table. *quantile regressions – dependent variable = borrowing*

	Bootstrap (method: residuals)		
	$\theta = 0.25$	$\theta = 0.5$	$\theta = 0.75$
Constant	10.84* *(6.52)*	8.84* *(6.72)*	18.66* *(11.54)*
Investment	–0.65 *(–1.27)*	–0.29 *(–0.74)*	–0.38 *(–0.79)*
Past borrowing	–0.55* *(–28.55)*	–0.61* *(–28.19)*	–0.41* *(–13.21)*
Self-financing capacity	–0.49 *(–1.15)*	–0.29 *(–0.89)*	0.04 *(0.12)*
Past debt	–1.65* *(–7.08)*	–1.39* *(–7.74)*	–2.86* *(–12.75)*
Interest rate level	–0.09 *(–0.86)*	0.07 *(0.66)*	0.32* *(2.24)*
R^2	0.19	0.18	0.33

Note: t-ratios in parentheses. All regressions include time fixed effects. * means that a coefficient is statistically significant at the 5% level of significance.
Source: G. Dufrénot, P. Frouté and C. Schalck (2010), "The French Regions' Borrowing Behaviours – How heterogeneous are they?", Banque de France, Working Paper no. 289.
Could this methodology be relevant in the case of legal certainty?

2.3. *Quantile regressions and legal certainty*

In the case of a comparative analysis of legal certainty, the use of quantile regressions may be very relevant. The use of quantiles enables to address two different issues.

First, quantile regressions methodology enables to address heterogeneity issues by assessing if significant identified variables are common among the different legal system governing real estate transactions. Second, they help to assess whether their impacts differ across countries. Indeed, contrary to small area estimates or contrary to traditional analysis quantile regressions give the elasticities the possibility to differ between quantiles. We can distinguish the different individuals in each quantile and then make different quantiles correspond with different legal systems or different kind of transactions.

Another main advantage of quantile regressions is the fact that they are not too much data intensive. Indeed, you do not have to distinguish sub-samples for running regressions. The analysis is made with the whole sample; it is only the focus on the chosen representative individuals that changes. This enables to use this methodology to rather small samples.

The main drawback is common with all the empirical methodologies. The quality of the results depends on the quality and on the relevance of the data. That is why, before being able to begin a quantitative analysis one has to carefully and fully encompass the issues especially when looking at legal matters.

3. Conclusion: discussion of the two methodologies and further research

This critical analysis of the main methodologies employed to overcome the weakness of the sample size of the data shows that in terms of international comparison of different legal systems, the methodologies used by the World Bank that belongs to the family of small area estimations are not appropriate for dealing with comparison of different legal systems. Indeed, those methodologies assume that there exists a common underlying generating process for the data. On a descriptive perspective, this approach is convenient, but on a normative ground, assuming the existence of an underlying model to be followed by all countries regardless of their legal system is too strong an assumption. The criticism can be extended to all quantitative techniques that are using a single framework to run comparative analysis.

In this respect, the technique of quantile regressions seems more promising because it allows to better take into account the heterogeneity of behaviours. Small area estimations assume that the same variables will cause the same effects as elasticities are constant while the quantile regressions allow these elasticities to vary across quantiles. Depending on the individuals, the countries or the considered regions, the same variables may therefore have different elasticities. In other words the same components: characteristics of the files, characteristics of the defendants etc., may be treated differently and as a result they may generate different outcomes.

However, the selection of relevant variables remains an essential prerequisite and requires a thorough understanding of legal systems before conducting any quantitative analysis of the effects of law. This is what provides this book on the question of legal certainty in real estate transactions.

At the end of this section, it is possible to identify some interesting insights for future works. The most promising method for dealing with small sample issues is the quantile regressions methodology because of its non normative perspective. Nevertheless, the methodology requires having access to files that are sufficiently representative of the activity of jurisdictions. The ideal number of files would 30 per country but a panel approach may enable to diminish this number thanks to the temporal dimension of the panel. For each of this file one has to select all the relevant components of the file: characteristics of the transaction (price, quality of the good, situation of the good…), characteristics of the parties (professionals, wealth…), characteristics of the proceedings (length, qualification of the legal facts, notaries, non notaries…) characteristics of the law (civilian law, common law…). The description of all those characteristics must be the deepest as possible. Variable can be quantitative, qualitative, dummies (0 or 1: existence or non existence for instance)… The idea is then to use these variable to asses a variable of interest: probability of litigation, probability of failure, amount for the compensation etc. That is to say, all the quantitative elements that may have a link with the notion of legal certainty.

For the chosen variable of interest, we will run the quantile regressions to study if the different characteristics may vary amongst the different quantiles. For instance, are the low observed litigation probabilities influenced differently by specific elements? Then, we will have a look at those elements in order to see if they are linked with a specific proceeding or a specific legal system. The perspective is empirical. It has two main dimensions. First, it enables to question the normative legal notions in order to know if, on a practical view, the desired effects are observed. Second, it may reveal some unexpected or counter-intuitive features of the legal system. In such cases, a second step would be to understand more deeply what kind of behaviours are at the origin of such observations.

These perspectives seem rather promising, but for this methodology to be used, it is necessary to have a full access to file in order not to forget important elements to fully encompass the heterogeneity of legal system. It is what we have missed in our study. But we hope to be able to have access to such data in the future in order to better empirically address the issue of legal certainty.

4. References

D'Orey V. and Koenker R. [1987], "Computing regression quantiles", *Applied statistics*, no. 36, pp. 383–393.

Dufrénot G., Frouté P. and Schalck C. [2010], "The French Regions' Borrowing Behaviours – How heterogeneous are they?", *Banque de France*, Working Paper no. 289.

Elbers C., Lanjouw J.and Lanjouw P. [2003], "Micro-level estimation of poverty and inequality", *Econometrica*, no. 71, pp. 355–364.

Isaki C. and Fuller W. [1982], "Survey design under the regression superpopulation model", *Journal of the American Statistical Association*, no. 77, pp. 89–96.

Isidro C.M., [2010], *Intercensal updating of small areas estimates*, PHD thesis in statistics, Massey University, Palmerston North, New Zealand.

Koenker R. [1994], "Confidence intervals for regression quantiles", *Asymptotic statistics*, pp. 349–359.

Koenker R. and Bassett G. [1978], "Regression Quantiles", *Econometrica*, vol 46 no. 1, pp. 33–50.

Koenker R. and Bassett G. [1982], "Robust Tests for Heteroscedasticity Based on Regression Quantiles," *Econometrica*, vol 50 no. 1, pp. 43–61.

NSCB [2005], *Estimation of the local poverty in the Philippines*, National Statistical Coordination Board, Philippines.

Rao J.N.K. [2003], *Small Area Estimation*, Wiley Series in Methodology, New York.

Skinner C.J., Holt D. and Smith T.M.F. [1989], *Analysis of complex survey data*, John Wiley, Chichester.

You Y. and Rao J.N.K. [2002], "A pseudo-empirical best linear unbiased prediction approach to small area estimation using survey weights", *Survey Methodology*, no. 30, pp. 431–439.

You Y., Rao J.N.K. and Kovacevic M. [2003], "Estimating fixed effects and variance components in a random intercept model using survey data", *Statistics Canada Symposium Series*-Proceedings.

CONCLUSION

Bertrand du Marais

COMPARATIVE LAW, "ECONOMIC ATTRACTIVENESS OF LAW" AND LEGAL CERTAINTY: SOME CONCLUDING REMARKS FROM A PILOT PROJECT*

As we stated in the Introduction and as mentioned by David Marrani in his "Introductory remarks on comparative law and interdisciplinarity", this book is the result of an ambitious project. Our initial aim was to assess the efficiency of legal instruments used to register real estate property transactions in order to provide legal certainty. We have addressed this issue through a multidisciplinary approach altogether combining legal with economic analysis and drawing a comparison between a Common Law country (using English and Welsh law) and a Civil Law country (France). As such, our project was also a project of comparative law in action, in similar sense as what is described by Esin Orücu.[1]

This project was built on a bet for a new methodology and on an assumption. The bet was to test a methodologsy which we could call "monographic and comparative economic impact assessment of law". The assumption was that legal certainty is deeply linked with local legal culture and is not a by-product of the standardisation of law and legal procedures. In this regard, this project is clearly a pilot project and should be assessed as such.[2]

But to address these issues and to try to draw some lessons from this research project, we first have to come upstream and to recall its genesis as a reaction to the World Bank *Doing Business* reports. The methodology and results of the World Bank gave birth to the "New comparative economics",[3] a recent school within economics, and to the "Legal

* I would like to thank David Marrani for his assistance and contribution to this conclusion.

1 Esin Orucu, 'A Project: Comparative Law in Action', in Esin Orücü & David Nelken (eds) *Comparative Law: A Handbook*, Hart Oxford 2007, pp. 435–449.

2 For Nelken [l]egal culture, in its most general sense, should be seen as one way of describing relatively stable patterns of legally-oriented social behaviour and attitudes. The identifying elements of legal culture range from facts about institutions such as the number and role of lawyers or the ways judges are appointed and controlled, to various forms of behavior such as litigation or prison rates, and, at the other extreme, more nebulous aspects of ideas, values, aspirations and mentalities. Like culture itself, legal culture is about who we are, not just what we do. David Nelken, 'Defining and Using the Concept of Legal Culture', in Esin Orücü & David Nelken (eds) *Comparative Law: A Handbook*, Hart Oxford 2007, pp. 109–133, esp. p. 113.

3 Djankov Simeon, Edward Glaeser, Rafael La Porta, Florencio Lopez-de-Silanes and Andrei Shleifer (2003), "The New Comparative Economics", *Journal of Comparative Economics*, 31, pp. 595–619.

origins theory",[4] which led to hot debates among economists as well as interdisciplinary exchanges between economists and comparative lawyers. Therefore, our analysis should also be put in perspective within these academic debates.

These concluding remarks will then be organized around the answers to three successive questions. Firstly, what "New comparative economics" does to comparative law? Or more precisely, what harm "New comparative economics" and its subsequent theories, such as "Legal origins" but also the economic assessment of the quality of law through indicators, may cause to comparative law? Secondly, what economics could do to comparative law? This second question then leads to what we may call the "Economic Attractiveness of Law" paradigm, bringing up an attempt to build new methodologies to compare the economic efficiency of legal instruments and institutions. Thirdly, what comparative law should bring to economics in order to ascertain legal certainty, which as described in this book, can be considered as a public good and a generator of economic growth?

1. What "(new comparative) economics" does to comparative law

The cooperation between economists and lawyers could bring an important and positive result because comparative legal analysis may help to solve some of the most difficult puzzles in economics, especially in development economics. One of these still unresolved questions is, as D. Acemoglu and J. Robinson phrased it in the title of their book, "Why nations fail"[5], whereas some have the same initial resources and human capital endowment as others which are booming? Since Ronald Coase and his follower Douglas North, economists have identified key factors for economic growth in the legal framework: the definition of property rights and the design of institutions and norms "as the rules of the game".

In order to address this issue, many economists have resorted to microeconomics and try identifying through theoretical model how law and institutions could frame the incentives for economic agents to act and then how this could lead to partial equilibrium. Others have conducted empirical studies, building econometric correlations between economic outcomes and the use of certain legal instruments or institutions. These empirical studies are mostly addressing a narrow issue with databases which are comprehensive but usually built for a specific country only. Therefore, if both of these methodologies bring extremely valuable results as to the interaction between law and economics, they are of little help for comparisons across jurisdictions.

Therefore, another trend has developed in economics in the last decade towards the use of synthetic numerical indicators in order to compare the relative efficiency of national legal instruments and institutions.

Of course, using abstract, synthetic numerical indicators in order to capture complex reality and to allow international comparison has always been commonplace in

4 Glaeser Edward, Andrei Shleifer (2002), "Legal Origins", 117 *Q. J. Econ.* p. 1193, 2002.

5 Daron Acemoglu, James A. Robinson, *Why nations fail – The origin of power, prosperity and poverty*, New York, Crown Business Book, 2012, 529 pp.

economics. However, the use of synthetic numerical indicators in order to assess the characteristics of legal instruments sparkled in economics with the work of the "Law and finance" group, especially after their seminal article bearing this title.[6]

The essence of this methodology is to build a large database combining, on the one hand, professional respondents' surveys about duration and cost of legal procedures, and on the other hand, the coding of laws through a binary technique (0 if a certain legal instrument is absent in a certain jurisdiction, 1 if it is present). The ultimate goal is to assess if such national legal framework offers certain legal instrument or institutions deemed conducive to growth according to an ex-ante economic model.

After the publication of several papers by the "Law and Finance" group under the intellectual chairmanship of Harvard economist A. Shleifer, this approach was then duplicated at worldwide level and across several legal regimes by the World Bank *Doing Business* project. It is not the purpose of these concluding remarks to describe in depth the *Doing Business* methodology which is addressed in several chapters of this book. Suffice to notice that, first, this methodology has been widely criticized, and not only by lawyers[7] and second that, despite its intrinsic flaws, the *Doing Business* project has been continuing year after year for more than a decade.[8] It is now one of the World Bank flagships and most circulated reports. Moreover, the *Doing Business* "project has passed from being a data source and research tool to playing role in the political economy of development policy. "[9]

Along with the *Doing Business* project, the "Law and Finance" team initiated the "New comparative economics"[10] and its subsequent theory "Legal origins".[11] This school of thoughts then initiated a sort of direct confrontation with comparative law, if not dispossessing it from its rationale as well as depriving it from its analytical and normative function. "New Comparative economics" may well constitute an irruption of classical microeconomics into comparative law. As a matter of fact, and to summarize it at the expense of some simplification, the "New comparative economics" papers describe the subtle balance between arbitrary decisions and free will that characterizes the level of Rule of Law as a trade off between two extremes – state expropriation called dictatorship and private expropriation called disorder. Then, a move towards more control over "disorder" should be done at the cost of more state control, and "a crucial determinant of

6 La Porta, Rafael; Florencio Lopez-De-Silvanes; Andrei Shleifer and Robert W. Vishny (1998), "Law and Finance", *Journal of Political Economy*, 106 (6), pp. 1113–1155.

7 Ménard Claude, Bertrand du Marais (2008), "Can We Rank Legal Systems According to Their Economic Efficiency?", *Washington University Journal of Law and Policy*, St Louis, Miss., Vol. 26, 2008, pp. 55–80.

8 See the debate between comparative law practitioners and academics R. Beauchard, C. Boisman, K. Davis and R. Michaels and World Bank economist C. Geginat: "Legal origins, *Doing Business*, and rule of law indicators: the economic evaluation of legal systems, *Proceedings of the Annual Meeting*, American Society of International Law, Vol.105 (March 23–26, 2011), pp. 37–60.

9 Besley Timothy (2015), "Law, Regulation, and the Business Climate: The Nature and Influence of the World Bank Doing Business Project", *The Journal of Economic Perspectives*, Vol. 29, No. 3, pp. 99–120 at 100.

10 Djankov Simeon, Edward Glaeser, Rafael La Porta, Florencio Lopez-de-Silanes and Andrei Shleifer (2003), "The New Comparative Economics", *Journal of Comparative Economics*, 31, pp. 595–619.

11 Glaeser Edward, Andrei Shleifer (2002), "Legal Origins", 117 *Q. J. Econ.* p. 1193, 2002.

institutional efficiency is the marginal effectiveness of dictatorship in reducing disorder".[12]

A corollary of this approach is the "Legal origins theory". This subsequent theory is a move from "New comparative economics" analytical grid and positive assumptions to a normative approximation. Briefly summarized (and therefore somewhat caricatured), the "Legal origins" theory infers several results. First, Civil and Common law traditions still influences greatly the current legal framework and institutional settings of each jurisdiction. Second, Common law is more conducive to growth for at least two main reasons: investors – and especially minority shareholders – are better protected and judges are more independent from state attempt to expropriate or bully private entrepreneurs.

These two theories – "New comparative economics" and "Legal origins" – generated, at least, a great interest for numerical index in order to compare the "quality" of business law among economists, but also among the investors' community, therefore making true the prevision of Justice Holmes, "For the rational study of the law the black letter man may be the man of the present, but the man of the future is the man of statistics and the master of economics."[13]

Powerful and influential as these theories may have been in early 2000s, they've gradually faded within the academic and policy design debates. However, this gradual eclipse was not due to a decrease in relevance. On the contrary, the legal metric and the binary coding methodology initiated by the LLSV team as well as their "Legal origins" normative approach passed into politics and business. They are so deeply embedded in decision makers beliefs that synthetic indexes assessing the supposed relative "quality" of national laws are now commonplace, if not commons sense. Theses indicators and rankings constitute the raw materials for many information services especially related to investment decisions such as financial rating agencies,[14] credit scoring, foreign direct investment (FDI) and the like. Therefore, synthetic indexes exert a powerful normative effect (e.g. *Doing Business*) with a view to spreading standardized law and institutions.[15]

The appeal of this methodology led to a large stream of economic literature that some called – either positively or negatively – "Numerical comparative law"[16], "Large-Sample, Quantitative Research Designs" for Comparative Law[17] or "Empirical comparative

12 Ibid. note 12 at p. 614.

13 Oliver Wendell Holmes, Jr., "The Path of the Law", 10 *Harvard Law Review* 457, 469 (1897).

14 Du Marais, Bertrand, Conac, Pierre-Henri, Piquemal, Alain and Froute, Philippe, "Rating the Law: How financial rating agencies are assessing the legal risks of financial transactions" in P. Nobel (dir.), *Law and Economics of Risk in Finance*, Schulthess, Zürich 2007, pp. 15–34.

15 Davis, Kevin, Angelina Fisher, Benedict Kingsbury, and Sally Engle Merry, (2011) "Indicators as a Technology of Global Governance", *IILJ Working Paper* 2010/2 Rev Finalized 08/02/2011, (www.iilj.org) or (2012), *Law and Society Review*, 46:1, pp. 71–104.

16 Siems, Mathias M. (2005), "Numerical Comparative Law: Do We Need Statistical Evidence in Law in Order to Reduce Complexity?", 13 *Cardozo Journal of International and Comparative Law*, vol. 13.

17 Spamann, Holger. (2009), "Large-Sample, Quantitative Research Designs for Comparative Law?", vol. 57, pp. 797–810.

law"[18] or "Comparative Law by Numbers".[19] This trend led to breakthroughs in identifying the differences in economic efficiency between jurisdictions but to some controversies in the comparative law community.

Indeed, it produces a major disruption in comparative law, not any more considered as an understanding of "*alterité*" (as mentioned in this book by D. Marrani following Legrand and other thinkers of legal comparison) but as a raw material for economic testing which then helps to develop a normative discourse on how national legal framework should be drafted in order to maximize efficiency. Therefore, to our first question "What "New comparative economics" does to comparative law?" we should answer that both this theory and the "legal origins" theory hit a major blow to comparative law, making it somewhat obsolete for policy design and investment decision making. Now, let us answer the second one, "What economics could do to comparative law: the "Economic attractiveness of law" approach and methodology".

2. What economics could bring to comparative law: the "economic attractiveness of law" approach and methodology

Contrary to these attempts to format different legal frameworks and institutions into the same metric, our purpose, as stated in the "Economic attractiveness of Law" Research program initiated in the years 2004–2007, is to reverse the *Doing Business* methodological approach and to work the other way round. This *Doing Business* methodology starts by computing, in each national legal system, the distance between the national legal reality and a predesigned model, built according to an ex-ante theory of the influence of Law on business. Then it compares the results at worldwide level in order to test, thanks to simple econometrics, economic theories about the relationships between law and growth. More specifically it contributes to confirm that a specific legal pattern or a standardized legal framework – or even a certain legal tradition – are more conducive to business and therefore would attract more foreign direct investments (FDI).

Our research strategy is, on the contrary, to identify the way each legal system, naturally, would elicit – or refrain – growth, and especially would attract or repel FDI because of inherent causes of economic efficiency or inefficiency. I call this approach "Economic attractiveness of Law", because attractiveness, although sometime a construct, is more often the result of a combination of gifts from the nature and of the context in which these natural dispositions are assessed.

So our approach – and the pilot project which gave birth to this book – put legal comparative studies at first and upfront. This initial step should be conducted in order to abide as much as possible by best practices in legal comparison. That is to say that this initial comparative step should be a dialog, a real, profound and unconstrained dialog

18 Spamann, Holger, (2015), "Empirical comparative law", *Annual Review of Law and Social Science*, Vol. 11, pp. 131–153.

19 Michaels, Ralph (2009), "Comparative Law by Numbers? Legal Origins Thesis, *Doing Business* Reports, and the Silence of Traditional Comparative Law", *The American Journal of Comparative Law*, 2009, Vol. 57.

between lawyers – both academics *and* practitioners, in order to mutually understand their legal culture but also – as stated by D. Marrani and now citing P. Legrand, in order to assess their "*mentalité*" (or "the underlying cognitive framework – of the unconscious of law") and in order to contrast their practices with "an empathy for alterity".[20]

But this approach is not pure and mere legal comparative studies. As a matter of fact, this initial step should be conducted in the presence of economists. Firstly, while witnessing this legal dialog, economists will be able to more precisely specify their variables, both dependant and independent and then be able to reduce the importance of what is often called "opportunistic behaviour" in economic literature. Secondly, this dialog will help economists to identify, if possible, the "modal" legal scheme, that is to say the most often used legal instrument to carry out a specific business transaction in each national legal culture. In our project, one of the puzzling results of this comparative dialogue stage was to stress that "legal certainty" – our dependent variable – did not have the same signification or meaning in France or in England. Its meaning is different in the different legal culture across the Channel ...

The main result of this comparative dialogue stage was to answer the following question: "in order to handle such specific business issue, how each legal culture is doing?" Rather than answering the question behind the *Doing Business* methodology: "in order to handle such specific business issue, does each national legal culture offer the same set of legal instruments and institutions?" Therefore, our approach is clearly connected to the "functional method" of comparative Law[21]

Then comes the efficiency testing of the legal instruments and institutions at stake, with economic analytical tools such as cost – benefit analysis but also econometrics and the like. In this second stage, economics is not a mere computational tool, used to test ex-ante assumptions which would have been invented by lawyers. The purpose of this stage is really to test and to refine economic models and theory. For instance, in the pilot project which led to this book, the economic models to be tested may be numerous, ranging from transaction costs theories (to analyse which legal institution brings less transaction costs) to public economics and regulation theory (e.g.: is a regulated profession more or less efficient than competing private practitioners?). In this stage, the more this economics analysis resort to official statistics and data, the better. In previous papers, we already have pointed at the limitations brought by perception surveys, albeit submitted to independent and learned respondents.[22]

In a third stage, the results of these efficiency tests should be confronted to a dialog between lawyers and economists. Such a dialog is necessary for analytical purposes – in order to refine the economic modelling but also to increase the level of precision of the legal comparison – as well as for normative analysis. This interdisciplinary dialog is of

20 Legrand, Pierre (1996) "Comparer", *Revue internationale de droit comparé*, Vol. 48, n° 2, Avril-juin 1996. pp. 279–318; (1996) "How to compare now", *Legal Studies*, 16, 1996, pp. 232–242.

21 Michaels, Ralf (2006), "Chapter 10. The Functional Method of Comparative Law", in Mathias Reimann and Reinhard Zimmermann (Ed.), *The Oxford Handbook of Comparative Law*, New York, Oxford University Press, 2006, pp. 339–382.

22 Ménard Claude, Bertrand du Marais (2008), "Can We Rank Legal Systems According to Their Economic Efficiency?", *Washington University Journal of Law and Policy*, St Louis, Miss., Vol. 26, 2008, pp. 55–80.

great value. As stressed by Nelken, 'Given the extent of overlap between disciplines, interdisciplinary work may also be easier to do than it is sometimes made to seem.'[23] It may also lead to valuable normative assessment, because the economic testing shows *where* each legal system develops institutions and legal instruments that bring economic efficiency or inefficiency in order to address a specific business need. In terms of policy recommendation, the result of our "monographic and comparative economic impact assessment of law" is much more nuanced, but more implementable than assigning a good or bad mark. The first approach suggests *where* and *what* to reform in the existing legal culture, rather than suggesting an overall reform to implement an external standard and then concentrating on *how* to reform.

In this regard, economics brings a major contribution to comparative impact assessment of law: either empirically by quantifying the impact of law or theoretically by identifying the incentives schemes derived from the implementation of law. After answering our second question "What economics could bring to comparative law: the "Economic attractiveness of law" approach and methodology", it is now time to consider our last one, "What comparative law should do to economics: legal certainty and the "jurisdiversity" approach".

3. What comparative law should do to economics: legal certainty and the "jurisdiversity" approach

Working in comparative law (or legal studies), or working as a comparative lawyer has more or less always been a question of analysing the law of (usually western) countries and their similarities. Notions of unification, harmonisation and convergence have been at the forefront of the traditional text books on the subject. But behind the thin layers of the 'text' and the similarities that may be deciphered between the 'texts' of different countries, hide a more diverse plurality, a more accurate diversity. Often disregarded as such, because of the drama it causes, mainly the intellectual incapacity of some comparative lawyers as well as decision makers to apprehend complexity, the jurisdiversity has an interdisciplinary dimension, because of 'contexts', in the day to day development of laws…

My approach, as embodied in this book, is that jurisdiversity, far form being an impediment to economic growth, brings on the contrary more efficiency into international transactions. This opinion comes both from a criticism of the legal standardization induced by the "Legal origins" theory and the actual influence of World Bank *Doing Business* project. It comes also from the definitions of Legal certainty we have identified in this book.

As a matter of fact, the *Doing Business* reports and all the synthetic numerical indicators measuring the "quality of law" convey a theoretic model according to which there exists a specific pre-existing pattern – or standard – of laws and institutions more efficient for business and economic growth than any other patterns. This efficient pattern

[23] David Nelken, 'Comparative Law at a Cross-roads' in Esin Örücü & David Nelken (eds) *Comparative Law: A Handbook*, Hart Oxford 2007, pp. 1–13.

maybe inspired by Anglo-American Common Law as "Legal origins" literature points out.

But legal standardization may also be a pattern that derives from other economic theory which may by chance be embodied in the legal or institutional framework of some existing jurisdictions, or not. This assumption of an ideal legal standard is then supported by at least three other economic theoretic arguments which are present in the background of *Doing Business* and "Legal origins".

First of all, the economic theory of "regulatory competition" *à la* Tiebout[24] should lead to the standardization of law and institutions. If, in the market for FDI locations, the suppliers of law (regulators and legislators of each jurisdiction) compete with each other, then if competition is pure and perfect, economic theory tells us that the market will converge towards a unique good supplied at the minimum cost. Secondly and in the same token, pure and perfect competition supposes homogeneity of products, i.e. here homogeneity of the national legal and institutional setting. Thirdly, a normative conception of transaction costs economics should induce a unique legal standard, so as to save foreign investors the costs of transposing contracts and by laws but also corporate governance statutes, etc. in order to settle in a new jurisdiction.

However these economic theories implying legal standardization are subject to harsh criticisms. Firstly, the "regulatory competition" theory has been strongly criticized. Secondly, the pure and perfect competition model applied to the market for jurisdiction should push "suppliers" of legal framework (i.e. competing jurisdictions) to differentiate in order to frame the market into "niches" where each jurisdiction has competitive advantages. Finally, we observe that standardizing law or importing "legal transplants" impose *transition* costs that may exceed *transaction* costs but which are not imposed on the same parties to a FDI transaction. *Transition* costs are usually born by the whole society of the investment recipient country – as shown in the transition from Communism in Central and Eastern Europe. At least, *transition* costs are supported by the local party to a FDI transaction. On the contrary *transaction* costs are usually shared by both parties, and at least partly supported by the foreign investor.

Nonetheless, our major criticism against "Legal origins" and against the tendency towards standardization of Law stems from the very notion of "Legal certainty" and its connection with jurisdiversity. This criticism is based on the assumption that legal certainty is best achieved, and then business operations and economic growth are best secured, when both parties to a transaction use a legal framework which is closely connected with the local legal and institutional framework. Or, to phrase it in another way, legal transplants and standardized law provide a superficial – if not misleading – legal certainty to both parties. Therefore, contrary to "Legal origins" theory, contrary to *Doing Business* implicit recommendations and contrary to the daily use of synthetic numerical indicators of the quality of law, jurisdiversity is an *asset* for economic growth rather than an impediment.

24 See Tiebout, Charles, "A Pure Theory of Local Expenditures", *Journal of Political Economy*, vol. 64, 1956, pp. 416–424.

Several chapters of this book have addressed and defined legal certainty. Getting back to its definition as a legal concept –then close to the definition of the Rule of Law, as R. Lanneau suggests in the Chapter "What is legal certainty? A theoretical essay"- we can see that what R. Lanneau calls "procedural legal certainty" and "material legal certainty" are not only abstract qualities that could be supplied by any off-the-ground legal framework. On the contrary, these qualities are closely interwoven with the local legal culture. The third element of legal certainty ("certainty in the efficacy of the law" as R. Lanneau phrases it) may also be called "functional legal certainty" as it is the certainty provided by the legal framework in order to reduce risks and uncertainty arising in the reality (such as completion risks, *force majeure*, etc.). This third component of legal certainty is moreover a construct of the local legal culture, since the need to resort to law (rather than to an economic substitute such as insurance schemes) in order to suppress a specific source of uncertainty is the result of a cultural demand and the product of local specific cognitive mechanisms.

To give an example from this book; let us consider two parties involved in a transnational real estate transaction, across the Channel. Even if the lending contract – or even the purchase contract, a rarer case – is a pure template abiding by international standards, the French party buying a property in the City of London will have to remember that the transaction will imply as a background the freedom of contract and the sanctity of agreements doctrines (See the Chapter of Y. Farah "Contractual Certainty under English Contract Law"). On the same token, the British investor buying the same kind of property in La Défense business area near Paris will have to remember the "*ordre public*" provision that will govern the contract even if they are not stated within the contract itself.

4. Next steps

In a way, our book is a good illustration of Nelken statement:

> "It is important to note that interdisciplinary collaboration can take different forms. A discipline such as economics finds itself in symbiosis with law even, or especially when, its techniques are different."[25]

The main result of the project is of great significance but limited scope: for large real estate property transactions with professional use, on each side of the Channel, investors do not care about the legal institutions involved insofar as the main driver of their investment decisions is a financial portfolio approach and their counterparts – either a single French civil law notary or a score of solicitors and various consultants – succeed in doing their best efforts to keeping costs and delays within the same magnitude and in providing legal certainty. As mentioned in our introductory chapter, this observation is

25 Ibid, note 10.

of a great significance, for the investors' community but also fort the legal professions involved.

However, we should confess as mentioned that this observation is still of limited scope. Due to various constraints –limited time and resources devoted to the research and moreover administrative difficulties to keep the project and the team consistent over time – we could not go deeper into the data gathering as we would have liked. Therefore we could only give a hint at economic modelling. Resorting to a few interviews was then expedient, yet frustrating since it was mirroring the *Doing Business* methodology. This leads, however, to one policy recommendation and one policy assessment.

The policy recommendation is a call to public institutions in order to develop harmonized legal and judicial statistics. Of course, as P Frouté demonstrates in his chapter "An Assessment of Theoretical Proposals to Deal with Heterogeneous Small Samples", the lack of official statistics available at a significant aggregated level may be compensated by an access to a small sample of existing cases filed into Courts' dockets or in notaries' and lawyers' offices. However this access raises many issues such as business secrecy, protection of personal data, etc. Nonetheless, this is the kind of data collection and research that should go on in the future.

The policy assessment is that, given the time devoted in our methodology to the comparative dialogue stage, our methodology may only do for researches dealing with a small sample of countries and targeted at a limited number of business issues. But this modest approach may be more relevant and surely not more costly then supporting huge international teams to maintain worldwide databases whose accuracy is constantly put into question.

IUS COMMUNE EUROPAEUM

A peer-reviewed book series in which the common foundations of the legal systems of the Member States of the European Union are the central focus.

The *Ius Commune Europaeum* series includes horizontal comparative legal studies as well as studies on the effect of treaties within the national legal systems. All the classic fields of law are covered. The books are published in various European languages under the auspices of METRO, the Institute for Transnational Legal Research at Maastricht University.

Recently published:
Volume 134: *Europe at the Edge of Pluralism*, D. Gozdecka and M. Kmak
Volume 135: *Cooperative Agreements between Public Authorities. The Influence of CJEU Case Law on National Legal Systems*, K. Wauters
Volume 136: *Common Core, PECL and DCFR: Could They Change Shipping and Transport Law?*, W. Verheyen, F.G.M. Smeele and M.A.I.H. Hoeks
Volume 137: *Who does What? On the Allocation of Competences in European Private Law*, B. Akkermans, J. Hage, N. Kornet and J.M. Smits
Volume 138: *The Nature of Mutual Recognition in European Law*. W. van Ballegooij
Volume 139: *Evidence in Contemporary Civil Procedure. Fundamental Issues in a Comparative Perspective*, C.H. van Rhee and A. Uzelac (eds.)
Volume 140: *The effect of D&O insurance on managerial risk taking*, Max Gaber
Volume 141: *Information and Notification Duties*, Ilse Samoy and Marco B. Loos
Volume 142: *The Application of the Theory of Efficient Breach in Contract Law. A Comparative Law and Economics Perspective*, Wenqing Liao
Volume 143: *A European Legal Framework for Nuclear Liability. Rethinking Current Approaches*, T. Heldt
Volume 144: *The Development of European Private Law in a Multilevel Legal Order*, E.A.G. Van Schagen
Volume 145: *Property Law Perspectives IV*, D. Gruyaert, E. Ramaekers and L. Rostill (eds.)
Volume 146: *The Citizen in European Private Law: Norm-setting, Enforcement and Choice*, C. Cauffman and J. Smits (eds.)

www.ingramcontent.com/pod-product-compliance
Ingram Content Group UK Ltd.
Pitfield, Milton Keynes, MK11 3LW, UK
UKHW051928100926
8556IPUK00022B/1433

9 781780 682983